Preface

In the past decade, the world has witnessed an extraordinary transformation in the realm of finance and technology. What began as a niche experiment with Bitcoin in 2009 has now blossomed into a dynamic ecosystem of digital currencies, decentralized finance, and blockchain innovation. This book serves as a Reference list of the current top 100 cryptocurrencies.

Digital currencies are no longer confined to the tech-savvy or speculative investors. They are reshaping industries, empowering the unbanked, and redefining how value is exchanged across borders. From the pioneering Bitcoin, often hailed as "digital gold," to the myriad of utility tokens fueling decentralized platforms, each currency tells a story of innovation, ambition, and resilience. This list seeks to act as a reference guide. It provides the top 100 based on Market Cap. Each entry is designed to equip readers with a snapshot of the coin's position in the rapidly changing market.

Digital Madness: A List of the top 100 Cryptocurrencies

Bitcoin (BTC)

- Also Known As: Digital Gold, ₿
- Launch Date: January 3, 2009
- Founder(s): Satoshi Nakamoto (anonymous individual or group)

Market Cap (2019-2024):

- 2019: $131 billion
- 2020: $349.7 billion
- 2021: $878 billion
- 2022: $320 billion
- 2023: $503 billion
- 2024: $1.9 trillion

Price (2019-2024):

- 2019: $7,240
- 2020: $28,944
- 2021: $47,754
- 2022: $16,547
- 2023: $26,507
- 2024: $97,178

Supply:

- Circulating Supply: ~19.5 million BTC
- Total Supply: 21 million BTC (capped supply)

Additional Information:

- Official Website: https://bitcoin.org
- Technology: Blockchain using SHA-256 hashing algorithm.
- Community Support: Largest global cryptocurrency community, active on GitHub, Reddit, and Twitter.
- Wallet Support: Compatible with most crypto wallets, including Ledger, Trezor, Exodus, and Mycelium.
- Security Features: Immutable blockchain, decentralized network, cryptographic security.

Notable Events:

- 2013: First $1,000 price milestone.
- 2021: El Salvador adopted BTC as legal tender.

Social Media Presence:

- Twitter: https://twitter.com/Bitcoin
- Reddit: https://www.reddit.com/r/Bitcoin

Ethereum (ETH)
- Also Known As: ETH
- Launch Date: July 30, 2015
- Founder(s): Vitalik Buterin, Gavin Wood, Anthony Di Iorio, Charles Hoskinson, Joseph Lubin, and Mihai Alisie

Market Cap (2019-2024):
- 2019: $14 billion
- 2020: $66 billion
- 2021: $390 billion
- 2022: $148 billion
- 2023: $210 billion
- 2024: $570 billion

Price (2019-2024):
- 2019: $133
- 2020: $738
- 2021: $3,960
- 2022: $1,203
- 2023: $1,736
- 2024: $4,312

Supply:
- Circulating Supply: ~120.4 million ETH
- Total Supply: Unlimited (issuance decreases over time under Proof-of-Stake).

Additional Information:
- Official Website: https://ethereum.org
- Technology: Blockchain supporting smart contracts and dApps, transitioned to Proof-of-Stake with Ethereum 2.0 (The Merge).
- Community Support: Highly active across GitHub, Reddit, Twitter, and Ethereum-focused forums.
- Wallet Support: Compatible with major wallets such as MetaMask, Trust Wallet, and hardware wallets like Ledger and Trezor.
- Security Features: Decentralized network with cryptographic security and Proof-of-Stake consensus.

Notable Events:
- 2021: London Hard Fork implemented EIP-1559, introducing fee burning.
- 2022: Transitioned to Proof-of-Stake with The Merge.

Social Media Presence:
- Twitter: https://twitter.com/ethereum
- Reddit: https://www.reddit.com/r/ethereum/

Tether (USDT)
- Also Known As: USDT, Tether Dollar
- Launch Date: October 6, 2014
- Founder(s): Brock Pierce, Reeve Collins, Craig Sellars

Market Cap (2019-2024):
- 2019: $4.1 billion
- 2020: $20.9 billion
- 2021: $78 billion
- 2022: $66 billion
- 2023: $83 billion
- 2024: $85 billion

Price (2019-2024):
- 2019: $1.00
- 2020: $1.00
- 2021: $1.00
- 2022: $1.00
- 2023: $1.00
- 2024: $1.00

Supply:
- Circulating Supply: ~85 billion USDT
- Total Supply: ~85 billion USDT

Additional Information:
- Official Website: https://tether.to
- Technology: ERC-20 token issued on Ethereum, also available on multiple blockchains including Tron and Solana.
- Community Support: Broad adoption across exchanges and financial platforms, active on Twitter and Telegram.
- Wallet Support: Supported by nearly all cryptocurrency wallets, including MetaMask, Trust Wallet, and hardware wallets like Ledger.
- Security Features: Regular audits to verify reserves backing the 1:1 USD peg.

Notable Events:
- 2021: Surpassed $78 billion in market cap, becoming the most widely used stablecoin.
- 2022: Played a critical role in liquidity during crypto market volatility.

Social Media Presence:
- Twitter: https://twitter.com/Tether_to
- Telegram: https://t.me/tether_to

Solana (SOL)
- Also Known As: SOL
- Launch Date: March 2020
- Founder(s): Anatoly Yakovenko, Greg Fitzgerald

Market Cap (2019-2024):
- 2019: Not Applicable
- 2020: $96 million
- 2021: $60 billion
- 2022: $12 billion
- 2023: $15 billion
- 2024: $18 billion

Price (2019-2024):
- 2019: Not Applicable
- 2020: $0.78
- 2021: $171
- 2022: $14
- 2023: $19
- 2024: $29

Supply:
- Circulating Supply: ~416 million SOL
- Total Supply: ~558 million SOL

Additional Information:
- Official Website: https://solana.com
- Technology: High-performance blockchain using Proof-of-History (PoH) for scalability and low-latency transactions.
- Community Support: Large and active community on Twitter, Reddit, and Discord.
- Wallet Support: Compatible with wallets like Phantom, Sollet, and Ledger.
- Security Features: Advanced cryptography and a decentralized network of validators secure the platform.

Notable Events:
- 2021: Achieved an all-time high price of $260 in November during a period of massive DeFi and NFT adoption.
- 2023: Fully recovered from a series of network outages, introducing robust updates to enhance reliability.

Social Media Presence:
- Twitter: https://twitter.com/solana
- Discord: https://discord.com/invite/solana

XRP (XRP)

- Also Known As: Ripple
- Launch Date: 2012
- Founder(s): Chris Larsen, Jed McCaleb

Market Cap (2019-2024):
- 2019: $9.4 billion
- 2020: $10.7 billion
- 2021: $44.4 billion
- 2022: $18.1 billion
- 2023: $33.6 billion
- 2024: $39.2 billion

Price (2019-2024):
- 2019: $0.19
- 2020: $0.28
- 2021: $0.91
- 2022: $0.36
- 2023: $0.51
- 2024: $0.78

Supply:
- Circulating Supply: ~53 billion XRP
- Total Supply: 100 billion XRP (pre-mined)

Additional Information:
- Official Website: https://ripple.com/xrp
- Technology: Distributed Ledger Technology (Ripple Protocol Consensus Algorithm); not blockchain-based.
- Community Support: Strong institutional backing; active on forums and social media.
- Wallet Support: Compatible with wallets like Ledger, Trust Wallet, and Exodus.
- Security Features: Decentralized network of validators and cryptographic security for transactions.

Notable Events:
- 2018: Reached an all-time high price of $3.84.
- 2020: SEC filed a lawsuit alleging XRP is an unregistered security.
- 2023: Partial court ruling in favor of Ripple, declaring XRP not a security in secondary markets.

Social Media Presence:
- Twitter: https://twitter.com/Ripple (2.5M+ followers)
- Reddit: r/Ripple (350K+ members)

BNB (BNB)

- Also Known As: Binance Coin
- Launch Date: July 2017
- Founder(s): Changpeng Zhao (CZ), Binance Team

Market Cap (2019-2024):

- 2019: $2.3 billion
- 2020: $5.8 billion
- 2021: $96.1 billion
- 2022: $38.5 billion
- 2023: $51.7 billion
- 2024: $64.3 billion

Price (2019-2024):

- 2019: $13
- 2020: $37
- 2021: $526
- 2022: $244
- 2023: $332
- 2024: $416

Supply:

- Circulating Supply: ~153 million BNB
- Total Supply: 200 million BNB (subject to periodic burns)

Additional Information:

- Official Website: https://www.bnbchain.org
- Technology: Binance Smart Chain (BSC), a high-performance blockchain optimized for DeFi and smart contracts, operates in parallel with Binance Chain.
- Community Support: Large and active community, particularly among Binance exchange users; active on forums, Twitter, and Reddit.
- Wallet Support: Compatible with wallets like Trust Wallet, MetaMask, and Ledger.
- Security Features: Advanced cryptographic protections and decentralized BNB Chain validators secure the ecosystem.

Notable Events:

- 2020: Binance Smart Chain (BSC) launched, enabling smart contract functionality.
- 2021: BNB price surged during the rise of decentralized finance (DeFi) on BSC.

Social Media Presence:

- Twitter: https://twitter.com/BinanceChain (1M+ followers)
- Reddit: r/Binance (750K+ members)

Dogecoin (DOGE)

- Also Known As: DOGE, Meme Coin
- Launch Date: December 6, 2013
- Founder(s): Billy Markus, Jackson Palmer

Market Cap (2019-2024):

- 2019: $300 million
- 2020: $500 million
- 2021: $85 billion
- 2022: $9.3 billion
- 2023: $11.5 billion
- 2024: $14.8 billion

Price (2019-2024):

- 2019: $0.0024
- 2020: $0.0046
- 2021: $0.68 (all-time high in May 2021)
- 2022: $0.07
- 2023: $0.08
- 2024: $0.11

Supply:

- Circulating Supply: ~140 billion DOGE (2024 estimate)
- Total Supply: Unlimited (inflationary, with ~5 billion DOGE added annually)

Additional Information:

- Official Website: https://dogecoin.com
- Technology: Proof-of-Work (PoW) blockchain based on Litecoin's technology (Scrypt algorithm).
- Community Support: Highly active and passionate community; strong presence on social media platforms like Twitter and Reddit.
- Wallet Support: Compatible with wallets like Dogecoin Core, Trust Wallet, and Ledger.
- Security Features: Decentralized network secured by miners; resistant to certain attacks due to its large mining community.

Notable Events:

- 2021: Massive price surge fueled by social media, celebrity endorsements, and Elon Musk's tweets.
- 2023: Continued development under Dogecoin Foundation to improve scalability and use cases.

Social Media Presence:

- Twitter: https://twitter.com/dogecoin (3.5M+ followers)
- Reddit: r/dogecoin (2.5M+ members)

USD Coin (USDC)

- Also Known As: USDC, Stablecoin
- Launch Date: September 2018
- Founder(s): Circle and Coinbase (via the Centre Consortium)

Market Cap (2019-2024):

- 2019: $500 million
- 2020: $3.9 billion
- 2021: $42 billion
- 2022: $44 billion
- 2023: $25 billion
- 2024: $26 billion

Price (2019-2024):

- 2019-2024: $1.00 (pegged to USD)

Supply:

- Circulating Supply: ~26 billion USDC (2024 estimate)
- Total Supply: Not capped (issued as needed based on reserves)

Additional Information:

- Official Website: https://www.circle.com/usdc
- Technology: Ethereum-based ERC-20 token; also available on other blockchains like Solana, Algorand, and Polygon.
- Community Support: Widely adopted in the crypto and DeFi ecosystem; trusted for its transparency and regulation compliance.
- Wallet Support: Supported by most wallets, including MetaMask, Trust Wallet, and hardware wallets like Ledger.
- Security Features: Fully backed by reserve assets (cash and short-term U.S. Treasury bonds) with monthly attestations by third-party auditors.

Notable Events:

- 2021: Became the second-largest stablecoin after Tether (USDT).
- 2022: Circle pledged full transparency, publishing monthly reserve breakdowns to address regulatory concerns.
- 2023: Expanded multi-chain support and strengthened its position in the DeFi space.

Social Media Presence:

- Twitter: https://twitter.com/circle (500K+ followers)
- Reddit: r/usdc (Community discussions primarily integrated with larger crypto forums)

Cardano (ADA)

- Also Known As: ADA
- Launch Date: September 29, 2017
- Founder(s): Charles Hoskinson

Market Cap (2019-2024):

- 2019: $1.1 billion
- 2020: $5.6 billion
- 2021: $91 billion
- 2022: $11.8 billion
- 2023: $13.9 billion
- 2024: $17.4 billion

Price (2019-2024):

- 2019: $0.03
- 2020: $0.18
- 2021: $3.10 (all-time high in September 2021)
- 2022: $0.26
- 2023: $0.40
- 2024: $0.56

Supply:

- Circulating Supply: ~35 billion ADA (2024 estimate)
- Total Supply: 45 billion ADA (maximum cap)

Additional Information:

- Official Website: https://cardano.org
- Technology: Proof-of-Stake (PoS) blockchain with Ouroboros consensus mechanism.
- Community Support: Highly engaged global community with strong presence on Twitter, Reddit, and Discord.
- Wallet Support: Compatible with wallets like Daedalus (official), Yoroi, and hardware wallets like Ledger and Trezor.
- Security Features: Peer-reviewed academic research ensures robust and secure protocol development.

Notable Events:

- 2021: "Alonzo" upgrade introduced smart contracts, enabling DeFi and dApps on Cardano.
- 2022: "Vasil" hard fork improved network scalability and performance.
- 2023: Expanded interoperability through cross-chain developments with other ecosystems like Ethereum.

Social Media Presence:

- Twitter: https://twitter.com/Cardano (1.5M+ followers)
- Reddit: r/cardano (700K+ members)

Staked Ether (stETH)

- Also Known As: stETH
- Launch Date: December 2020
- Founder(s): Lido Finance Team

Market Cap (2019-2024):
- 2019: Not Applicable
- 2020: $100 million
- 2021: $6 billion
- 2022: $5.1 billion
- 2023: $15.3 billion
- 2024: $18.7 billion

Price (2019-2024):
- 2019: Not Applicable
- 2020: $730
- 2021: $3,680
- 2022: $1,200
- 2023: $1,840
- 2024: $2,100

Supply:
- Circulating Supply: ~8.9 million stETH (2024 estimate)
- Total Supply: Dynamic, increases as users stake ETH

Additional Information:
- Official Website: https://lido.fi
- Technology: Liquid staking derivative that represents staked ETH, earning rewards while remaining tradable and usable in DeFi.
- Community Support: Supported by a vibrant DeFi community with active discussions on Twitter, Discord, and Reddit.
- Wallet Support: Compatible with wallets like MetaMask, Trust Wallet, and Ledger.
- Security Features: Secured by Lido's smart contracts and audited by top blockchain security firms.

Notable Events:
- 2021: Emerged as the largest liquid staking solution for Ethereum.
- 2022: Maintained functionality through Ethereum's transition to Proof-of-Stake (The Merge).

Social Media Presence:
- Twitter: https://twitter.com/lidofinance (300K+ followers)
- Reddit: r/lidofinance (Active discussions on Ethereum staking and Lido protocol)

Shiba Inu (SHIB)
- Also Known As: SHIB, The Dogecoin Killer
- Launch Date: August 2020
- Founder(s): Ryoshi (pseudonymous)

Market Cap (2019-2024):
- 2019: Not Applicable
- 2020: $0.05 million
- 2021: $41 billion (all-time high in October 2021)
- 2022: $5.4 billion
- 2023: $6.3 billion
- 2024: $7.2 billion

Price (2019-2024):
- 2019: Not Applicable
- 2020: $0.00000001
- 2021: $0.000088
- 2022: $0.0000097
- 2023: $0.000011
- 2024: $0.000013

Supply:
- Circulating Supply: ~589 trillion SHIB
- Total Supply: 1 quadrillion SHIB (originally, but over 40% has been burned)

Additional Information:
- Official Website: https://shibatoken.com
- Technology: Ethereum-based ERC-20 token with a growing ecosystem, including ShibaSwap (DEX) and Shibarium (Layer 2 blockchain).
- Community Support: One of the largest and most passionate crypto communities; active on Twitter, Reddit, and Discord.
- Wallet Support: Compatible with MetaMask, Trust Wallet, Ledger, and more.
- Security Features: Operates as a decentralized token on Ethereum's robust blockchain.

Notable Events:
- 2021: Explosive growth, partly driven by social media and Elon Musk's indirect influence.
- 2022: Launch of ShibaSwap and plans for Shibarium, expanding utility beyond a meme token.

Social Media Presence:
- Twitter: https://twitter.com/Shibtoken (3.8M+ followers)
- Reddit: r/SHIBArmy (500K+ members)

Avalanche (AVAX)

- Also Known As: AVAX
- Launch Date: September 2020
- Founder(s): Emin Gün Sirer, Ava Labs

Market Cap (2019-2024):

- 2019: Not Applicable
- 2020: $0.1 billion
- 2021: $28 billion
- 2022: $4.9 billion
- 2023: $5.8 billion
- 2024: $7.2 billion

Price (2019-2024):

- 2019: Not Applicable
- 2020: $3.50
- 2021: $146 (all-time high in November 2021)
- 2022: $10.90
- 2023: $15.20
- 2024: $18.40

Supply:

- Circulating Supply: ~350 million AVAX (2024 estimate)
- Total Supply: 720 million AVAX (capped supply)

Additional Information:

- Official Website: https://avax.network
- Technology: High-performance blockchain platform with a unique Avalanche Consensus Protocol, designed for scalability and low-latency transactions.
- Community Support: Active community with strong developer engagement and social media presence.
- Wallet Support: Compatible with wallets like Avalanche Wallet, MetaMask, Trust Wallet, and Ledger.
- Security Features: Decentralized network with robust consensus mechanisms, ensuring security and reliability.

Notable Events:

- 2021: Surpassed $10 billion in total value locked (TVL) in its DeFi ecosystem.
- 2022: Partnered with Amazon Web Services (AWS) to drive blockchain adoption.

Social Media Presence:

- Twitter: https://twitter.com/avalancheavax (800K+ followers)
- Reddit: r/Avax (110K+ members)

TRON (TRX)

- Also Known As: TRX
- Launch Date: September 2017
- Founder(s): Justin Sun

Market Cap (2019-2024):

- 2019: $1.2 billion
- 2020: $1.6 billion
- 2021: $10.8 billion
- 2022: $5.1 billion
- 2023: $8.2 billion
- 2024: $9.6 billion

Price (2019-2024):

- 2019: $0.018
- 2020: $0.028
- 2021: $0.16
- 2022: $0.051
- 2023: $0.072
- 2024: $0.082

Supply:

- Circulating Supply: ~89 billion TRX
- Total Supply: ~100 billion TRX (maximum cap)

Additional Information:

- Official Website: https://tron.network
- Technology: Decentralized blockchain platform focused on content sharing, smart contracts, and decentralized applications (dApps).
- Community Support: Active community across social media, particularly in Asia, with strong developer and dApp ecosystem support.
- Wallet Support: Compatible with wallets like TronLink, Trust Wallet, and Ledger.
- Security Features: Delegated Proof-of-Stake (DPoS) consensus mechanism with 27 Super Representatives securing the network.

Notable Events:

- 2018: Acquired BitTorrent, integrating it into the TRON ecosystem.
- 2021: Expanded its DeFi and NFT ecosystem with projects like JustSwap and APENFT.
- 2023: Grew as a key player in the stablecoin market with its USDD stablecoin.

Social Media Presence:

- Twitter: https://twitter.com/trondao (1M+ followers)
- Reddit: r/Tronix (120K+ members)

Toncoin (TON)

- Also Known As: TON
- Launch Date: 2018
- Founder(s): Originally developed by Telegram; now maintained by the TON Foundation

Market Cap (2019-2024):
- 2019: Not Applicable
- 2020: Not Applicable
- 2021: $5.2 billion
- 2022: $8.7 billion
- 2023: $18.3 billion
- 2024: $20.5 billion

Price (2019-2024):
- 2019: Not Applicable
- 2020: Not Applicable
- 2021: $2.21
- 2022: $3.50
- 2023: $7.63
- 2024: $8.20

Supply:
- Circulating Supply: ~3.47 billion TON
- Total Supply: 5 billion TON (maximum cap)

Additional Information:
- Official Website: https://ton.org
- Technology: Layer-1 blockchain platform designed for scalability and cross-chain interoperability.
- Community Support: Strong association with Telegram's vast user base; active community engagement.
- Wallet Support: Compatible with wallets like Tonkeeper and Tonhub, and integrated into Telegram.
- Security Features: Decentralized network with robust consensus mechanisms.

Notable Events:
- 2018: Development initiated by Telegram, later transitioned to an open-source community project.
- 2023: Telegram endorsed TON as its official blockchain infrastructure, integrating Toncoin into its ecosystem.

Social Media Presence:
- Twitter: https://twitter.com/ton_blockchain (500K+ followers)
- Reddit: r/toncoin (150K+ members)

Wrapped stETH (WSTETH)

- Also Known As: WSTETH
- Launch Date: March 2022
- Founder(s): Lido Finance Team

Market Cap (2019-2024):

- 2019: Not Applicable
- 2020: Not Applicable
- 2021: Not Applicable
- 2022: $2.3 billion
- 2023: $6.5 billion
- 2024: $7.8 billion

Price (2019-2024):

- 2019: Not Applicable
- 2020: Not Applicable
- 2021: Not Applicable
- 2022: $1,210
- 2023: $1,830
- 2024: $2,120

Supply:

- Circulating Supply: ~3.2 million WSTETH (2024 estimate)
- Total Supply: Dynamic, mirrors the supply of stETH (determined by the amount of ETH staked).

Additional Information:

- Official Website: https://lido.fi
- Technology: Wrapped version of stETH, allowing precise DeFi compatibility by maintaining a fixed token-to-stETH conversion ratio.
- Community Support: Backed by Lido's active community with strong participation in DeFi and staking discussions.
- Wallet Support: Compatible with DeFi-friendly wallets such as MetaMask, Trust Wallet, and hardware wallets like Ledger.
- Security Features: Benefits from Lido's audited smart contracts and Ethereum's decentralized staking model.

Notable Events:

- 2022: Launched as a solution to improve DeFi integration for stETH.
- 2023: Gained traction as a key collateral asset in lending protocols like Aave and MakerDAO.

Social Media Presence:

- Twitter: https://twitter.com/lidofinance (300K+ followers)
- Reddit: r/lidofinance (Active community discussing Ethereum staking and Lido protocol).

Stellar (XLM)

- Also Known As: Lumens
- Launch Date: July 31, 2014
- Founder(s): Jed McCaleb, Joyce Kim

Market Cap (2019-2024):

- 2019: $1.1 billion
- 2020: $1.5 billion
- 2021: $9.1 billion
- 2022: $3.4 billion
- 2023: $4.2 billion
- 2024: $5.1 billion

Price (2019-2024):

- 2019: $0.06
- 2020: $0.13
- 2021: $0.73 (all-time high in May 2021)
- 2022: $0.11
- 2023: $0.12
- 2024: $0.14

Supply:

- Circulating Supply: ~27 billion XLM (2024 estimate)
- Total Supply: 50 billion XLM (reduced from 100 billion after a 2019 token burn)

Additional Information:

- Official Website: https://stellar.org
- Technology: Decentralized open-source blockchain for fast and low-cost cross-border payments.
- Community Support: Strong support from developers and enterprises focused on payment solutions; active presence on social platforms.
- Wallet Support: Compatible with Stellar-based wallets like Lobstr, and hardware wallets like Ledger.
- Security Features: Secured by the Stellar Consensus Protocol (SCP), designed for efficiency and resilience.

Notable Events:

- 2019: Burned 50 billion XLM to increase scarcity and focus on ecosystem development.
- 2021: Partnered with MoneyGram for blockchain-powered international payments.

Social Media Presence:

- Twitter: https://twitter.com/stellarorg (600K+ followers)
- Reddit: r/Stellar (220K+ members)

Polkadot (DOT)

- Also Known As: DOT
- Launch Date: May 2020
- Founder(s): Dr. Gavin Wood and Peter Czaban

Market Cap (2019-2024):
- 2019: Not Applicable
- 2020: Approximately $3.5B
- 2021: Approximately $30B
- 2022: Approximately $7B
- 2023: Approximately $10B
- 2024: Approximately $13.16B

Price (2019-2024):
- 2019: Not Applicable
- 2020: Opened at $2.90; closed at $8.00
- 2021: Opened at $8.00; closed at $26.72
- 2022: Opened at $26.72; closed at $4.37
- 2023: Opened at $4.37; closed at $5.93
- 2024: Opened at $5.93; current price: $9.04

Supply:
- Circulating Supply: Approximately 1.45 billion DOT
- Total Supply: Unlimited (inflationary model)

Additional Information:
- Official Website: polkadot.network
- Technology: Blockchain platform enabling interoperability between blockchains.
- Community Support: Active on Twitter and Reddit.
- Wallet Support: Compatible with Ledger, Trezor, and Polkadot.js.
- Security Features: Uses Nominated Proof-of-Stake (NPoS).

Notable Events:
- 2021: Introduction of Parachains, completing Polkadot 1.0.
- 2023: Announcement of Polkadot 2.0 by founder Gavin Wood.

Social Media Presence:
- Twitter: twitter.com/Polkadot
- Reddit: reddit.com/r/dot

Wrapped Bitcoin (WBTC)

- Also Known As: WBTC
- Launch Date: January 2019
- Founder(s): BitGo, Kyber Network, and Ren

Market Cap (2019-2024):

- 2019: Approximately $4.5M
- 2020: Approximately $1.1B
- 2021: Approximately $14.5B
- 2022: Approximately $7.8B
- 2023: Approximately $9.2B
- 2024: Approximately $13.55B

Price (2019-2024):

- 2019: Opened at $3,500; closed at $7,200
- 2020: Opened at $7,200; closed at $28,900
- 2021: Opened at $28,900; closed at $47,700
- 2022: Opened at $47,700; closed at $16,500
- 2023: Opened at $16,500; closed at $26,500
- 2024: Opened at $26,500; current price: $95,711

Supply:

- Circulating Supply: Approximately 141,000 WBTC
- Total Supply: Approximately 141,000 WBTC

Additional Information:

- Official Website: wbtc.network
- Technology: ERC-20 token representing Bitcoin on the Ethereum blockchain
- Community Support: Active on Twitter and Reddit
- Wallet Support: Compatible with major wallets like MetaMask and Ledger
- Security Features: Regular audits and proof of reserve

Notable Events:

- 2019: Launch of WBTC on Ethereum mainnet
- 2024: Coinbase announced delisting of WBTC effective December 19, 2024

Social Media Presence:

- Twitter: twitter.com/WrappedBTC
- Reddit: reddit.com/r/WrappedBitcoin

Chainlink (LINK)

- Also Known As: LINK
- Launch Date: September 2017
- Founder(s): Sergey Nazarov and Steve Ellis

Market Cap (2019-2024):
- 2019: Approximately $617M
- 2020: Approximately $1.3B
- 2021: Approximately $9.7B
- 2022: Approximately $3.5B
- 2023: Approximately $5.8B
- 2024: Approximately $11.56B

Price (2019-2024):
- 2019: Opened at $0.30; closed at $1.77
- 2020: Opened at $1.80; closed at $11.87
- 2021: Opened at $11.90; closed at $19.60
- 2022: Opened at $19.70; closed at $5.60
- 2023: Opened at $5.65; closed at $9.25
- 2024: Opened at $9.30; current price: $19.63

Supply:
- Circulating Supply: Approximately 626.85 million LINK
- Total Supply: 1 billion LINK

Additional Information:
- Official Website: chain.link
- Technology: Decentralized oracle network connecting smart contracts with real-world data
- Community Support: Active on Twitter and Reddit
- Wallet Support: Compatible with wallets like MetaMask and Ledger
- Security Features: Regular audits and bug bounty programs

Notable Events:
- 2023: Chainlink's social dominance reached 1.55%, the highest in 2024
- 2024: Integration with SWIFT for cross-chain interoperability

Social Media Presence:
- Twitter: twitter.com/chainlink
- Reddit: reddit.com/r/Chainlink

Wrapped Ether (WETH)

- Also Known As: WETH
- Launch Date: 2017
- Founder(s): Developed by the Ethereum community

Market Cap (2019-2024):

- 2019: Approximately $1.5B
- 2020: Approximately $5.0B
- 2021: Approximately $20.0B
- 2022: Approximately $10.0B
- 2023: Approximately $15.0B
- 2024: Approximately $12.41B

Price (2019-2024):

- 2019: Opened at $130; closed at $150
- 2020: Opened at $150; closed at $730
- 2021: Opened at $730; closed at $3,700
- 2022: Opened at $3,700; closed at $1,200
- 2023: Opened at $1,200; closed at $1,800
- 2024: Opened at $1,800; current price: $3,621.37

Supply:

- Circulating Supply: Approximately 3.38 million WETH
- Total Supply: Not capped

Additional Information:

- Official Website: weth.io
- Technology: ERC-20 token representing Ether (ETH) on the Ethereum blockchain
- Community Support: Active on Twitter and Reddit
- Wallet Support: Compatible with major wallets like MetaMask and Ledger
- Security Features: Smart contracts audited by the Ethereum community

Notable Events:

- 2017: Launch of WETH to facilitate ERC-20 token interactions
- 2024: Integration with Ethereum 2.0 staking mechanisms

Social Media Presence:

- Twitter: twitter.com/wrappedether
- Reddit: reddit.com/r/ethereum

Bitcoin Cash (BCH)

- Also Known As: BCH
- Launch Date: August 1, 2017
- Founder(s): Developed by a group of Bitcoin developers and miners

Market Cap (2019-2024):

- 2019: Approximately $3.5B
- 2020: Approximately $5.0B
- 2021: Approximately $10.0B
- 2022: Approximately $2.5B
- 2023: Approximately $4.0B
- 2024: Approximately $9.5B

Price (2019-2024):

- 2019: Opened at $150; closed at $200
- 2020: Opened at $200; closed at $350
- 2021: Opened at $350; closed at $500
- 2022: Opened at $500; closed at $150
- 2023: Opened at $150; closed at $250
- 2024: Opened at $250; current price: $519.31

Supply:

- Circulating Supply: Approximately 19.5 million BCH
- Total Supply: 21 million BCH (capped supply)

Additional Information:

- Official Website: bitcoincash.org
- Technology: Blockchain platform with larger block sizes for faster transactions
- Community Support: Active on Twitter and Reddit
- Wallet Support: Compatible with wallets like Ledger, Trezor, and Electron Cash
- Security Features: Proof-of-Work consensus mechanism

Notable Events:

- 2017: Hard fork from Bitcoin, creating Bitcoin Cash
- 2023: Price surge due to listing on institutional-backed exchange EDX Markets

Social Media Presence:

- Twitter: twitter.com/BitcoinCash
- Reddit: reddit.com/r/Bitcoincash

Sui (SUI)
- Also Known As: SUI
- Launch Date: May 3, 2023
- Founder(s): Developed by Mysten Labs

Market Cap (2019-2024):
- 2019: Not Applicable
- 2020: Not Applicable
- 2021: Not Applicable
- 2022: Not Applicable
- 2023: Approximately $10.07B
- 2024: Approximately $10.21B

Price (2019-2024):
- 2019: Not Applicable
- 2020: Not Applicable
- 2021: Not Applicable
- 2022: Not Applicable
- 2023: Opened at $0.94; closed at $3.44
- 2024: Opened at $3.44; current price: $3.27

Supply:
- Circulating Supply: Approximately 2.9 billion SUI
- Total Supply: Capped at 10 billion SUI

Additional Information:
- Official Website: sui.io
- Technology: Layer-1 blockchain platform designed for high throughput and low latency
- Community Support: Active on Twitter and Discord
- Wallet Support: Compatible with Sui Wallet and other major wallets
- Security Features: Utilizes the Move programming language for secure smart contracts

Notable Events:
- 2023: Mainnet launch on May 3
- 2024: Integration with major DeFi platforms

Social Media Presence:
- Twitter: twitter.com/SuiNetwork
- Discord: discord.com/invite/sui

Pepe (PEPE)
- Also Known As: PEPE
- Launch Date: April 2023
- Founder(s): Anonymous developers

Market Cap (2019-2024):
- 2019: Not Applicable
- 2020: Not Applicable
- 2021: Not Applicable
- 2022: Not Applicable
- 2023: Approximately $8.5B
- 2024: Approximately $8.1B

Price (2019-2024):
- 2019: Not Applicable
- 2020: Not Applicable
- 2021: Not Applicable
- 2022: Not Applicable
- 2023: Opened at $0.0000013; closed at $0.000019
- 2024: Opened at $0.000019; current price: $0.00001922

Supply:
- Circulating Supply: Approximately 420.69 trillion PEPE
- Total Supply: 420.69 trillion PEPE

Additional Information:
- Official Website: pepecoin.org
- Technology: ERC-20 token on the Ethereum blockchain
- Community Support: Active on Twitter and Reddit
- Wallet Support: Compatible with major wallets like MetaMask and Trust Wallet
- Security Features: Smart contracts audited by independent firms

Notable Events:
- 2023: Achieved a market cap of $8.5B within months of launch
- 2024: Integration with major decentralized exchanges

Social Media Presence:
- Twitter: twitter.com/pepecoineth
- Reddit: reddit.com/r/pepecoin

NEAR Protocol (NEAR)

- Also Known As: NEAR
- Launch Date: April 2020
- Founder(s): Alexander Skidanov and Illia Polosukhin

Market Cap (2019-2024):

- 2019: Not Applicable
- 2020: Approximately $1.2B
- 2021: Approximately $6.5B
- 2022: Approximately $3.8B
- 2023: Approximately $5.2B
- 2024: Approximately $8.1B

Price (2019-2024):

- 2019: Not Applicable
- 2020: Opened at $1.00; closed at $1.50
- 2021: Opened at $1.50; closed at $8.00
- 2022: Opened at $8.00; closed at $4.00
- 2023: Opened at $4.00; closed at $6.00
- 2024: Opened at $6.00; current price: $6.65

Supply:

- Circulating Supply: Approximately 1.22 billion NEAR
- Total Supply: Not capped

Additional Information:

- Official Website: near.org
- Technology: Layer-1 blockchain with sharding for scalability
- Community Support: Active on Twitter and Discord
- Wallet Support: Compatible with NEAR Wallet, MetaMask, and Ledger
- Security Features: Proof-of-Stake consensus mechanism

Notable Events:

- 2021: First phase of sharding implemented
- 2022: Closed a $500M funding round

Social Media Presence:

- Twitter: twitter.com/NEARProtocol
- Discord: discord.com/invite/near

Litecoin (LTC)

- Also Known As: Digital Silver
- Launch Date: October 7, 2011
- Founder(s): Charlie Lee

Market Cap (2019-2024):

- 2019: Approximately $3.5B
- 2020: Approximately $5.0B
- 2021: Approximately $10.0B
- 2022: Approximately $4.0B
- 2023: Approximately $7.0B
- 2024: Approximately $8.5B

Price (2019-2024):

- 2019: Opened at $30; closed at $40
- 2020: Opened at $40; closed at $70
- 2021: Opened at $70; closed at $150
- 2022: Opened at $150; closed at $60
- 2023: Opened at $60; closed at $100
- 2024: Opened at $100; current price: $119.97

Supply:

- Circulating Supply: Approximately 73 million LTC
- Total Supply: 84 million LTC (capped supply)

Additional Information:

- Official Website: litecoin.org
- Technology: Blockchain platform with faster transaction times and lower fees than Bitcoin.
- Community Support: Active on Twitter and Reddit.
- Wallet Support: Compatible with wallets like Ledger, Trezor, and Exodus.
- Security Features: Proof-of-Work consensus mechanism using Scrypt algorithm.

Notable Events:

- 2023: Litecoin's mining difficulty and hash rate reached all-time highs, indicating increased network security and miner participation.
- 2024: Grayscale Litecoin Trust filed multiple Form 8-Ks for unregistered equity sales, reflecting institutional interest.

Social Media Presence:

- Twitter: twitter.com/Litecoin
- Reddit: reddit.com/r/litecoin

Uniswap (UNI)
- Also Known As: UNI
- Launch Date: September 2020
- Founder(s): Hayden Adams

Market Cap (2019-2024):
- 2019: Not Applicable
- 2020: Approximately $500M
- 2021: Approximately $15B
- 2022: Approximately $5B
- 2023: Approximately $7.8B
- 2024: Approximately $7.86B

Price (2019-2024):
- 2019: Not Applicable
- 2020: Opened at $3.00; closed at $5.00
- 2021: Opened at $5.00; closed at $17.00
- 2022: Opened at $17.00; closed at $6.00
- 2023: Opened at $6.00; closed at $12.00
- 2024: Opened at $12.00; current price: $12.77

Supply:
- Circulating Supply: Approximately 615 million UNI
- Total Supply: 1 billion UNI

Additional Information:
- Official Website: uniswap.org
- Technology: Decentralized exchange protocol on the Ethereum blockchain.
- Community Support: Active on Twitter and Discord.
- Wallet Support: Compatible with MetaMask, Trust Wallet, and Ledger.
- Security Features: Smart contracts audited by multiple security firms.

Notable Events:
- 2023: Received a Wells notice from the SEC, indicating potential enforcement action.
- 2024: UNI token price surged over 50% following a revenue-sharing governance proposal.

Social Media Presence:
- Twitter: twitter.com/Uniswap
- Discord: discord.com/invite/Uniswap

UNUS SED LEO (LEO)

- Also Known As: LEO
- Launch Date: May 2019
- Founder(s): iFinex Inc.

Market Cap (2019-2024):

- 2019: Approximately $1.0B
- 2020: Approximately $1.2B
- 2021: Approximately $2.5B
- 2022: Approximately $3.0B
- 2023: Approximately $7.8B
- 2024: Approximately $8.0B

Price (2019-2024):

- 2019: Opened at $1.00; closed at $1.20
- 2020: Opened at $1.20; closed at $1.50
- 2021: Opened at $1.50; closed at $2.70
- 2022: Opened at $2.70; closed at $3.50
- 2023: Opened at $3.50; closed at $8.00
- 2024: Opened at $8.00; current price: $8.80

Supply:

- Circulating Supply: Approximately 924.67 million LEO
- Total Supply: 985.24 million LEO

Additional Information:

- Official Website: https://www.bitfinex.com
- Technology: Utility token for the iFinex ecosystem, operating on Ethereum and EOS blockchains.
- Community Support: Active on Twitter and Reddit.
- Wallet Support: Compatible with major wallets like MetaMask and Ledger.
- Security Features: Regular audits and compliance measures.

Notable Events:

- 2019: Launch of LEO token to cover financial shortfall.
- 2023: Achieved all-time high price of $8.97.

Social Media Presence:

- Twitter: https://twitter.com/bitfinex
- Reddit: https://reddit.com/r/bitfinex

Hedera (HBAR)
- Also Known As: HBAR
- Launch Date: August 2018
- Founder(s): Dr. Leemon Baird and Mance Harmon

Market Cap (2019-2024):
- 2019: Approximately $124 million
- 2020: Approximately $1.2 billion
- 2021: Approximately $3.5 billion
- 2022: Approximately $1.8 billion
- 2023: Approximately $2.5 billion
- 2024: Approximately $3.0 billion

Price (2019-2024):
- 2019: Opened at $0.12; closed at $0.03
- 2020: Opened at $0.03; closed at $0.05
- 2021: Opened at $0.05; closed at $0.29
- 2022: Opened at $0.29; closed at $0.08
- 2023: Opened at $0.08; closed at $0.12
- 2024: Opened at $0.12; current price: $0.239932

Supply:
- Circulating Supply: Approximately 33 billion HBAR
- Total Supply: 50 billion HBAR

Additional Information:
- Official Website: https://hedera.com
- Technology: Distributed ledger using Hashgraph consensus for high throughput and low latency.
- Community Support: Active on Twitter and Discord.
- Wallet Support: Compatible with wallets like Ledger, Atomic Wallet, and MyHbarWallet.
- Security Features: Asynchronous Byzantine Fault Tolerance (aBFT) consensus mechanism.

Notable Events:
- 2021: Hedera Governing Council allocated $5 billion in HBAR to ecosystem development initiatives.
- 2023: Over 100 products and services went live on the Hedera network, marking significant ecosystem growth.

Social Media Presence:
- Twitter: https://twitter.com/hedera
- Discord: https://discord.com/invite/hedera

Aptos (APT)

- Also Known As: APT
- Launch Date: October 12, 2022
- Founder(s): Avery Ching and Mo Shaikh

Market Cap (2019-2024):

- 2019: Not Applicable
- 2020: Not Applicable
- 2021: Not Applicable
- 2022: Approximately $1.2B
- 2023: Approximately $6.6B
- 2024: Approximately $6.7B

Price (2019-2024):

- 2019: Not Applicable
- 2020: Not Applicable
- 2021: Not Applicable
- 2022: Opened at $7.00; closed at $3.08
- 2023: Opened at $3.08; closed at $12.45
- 2024: Opened at $12.45; current price: $12.57

Supply:

- Circulating Supply: Approximately 534 million APT
- Total Supply: 1 billion APT

Additional Information:

- Official Website: aptosfoundation.org
- Technology: Layer-1 blockchain utilizing the Move programming language for scalability and security.
- Community Support: Active on Twitter and Discord.
- Wallet Support: Compatible with wallets like Petra and Martian.
- Security Features: Byzantine Fault Tolerant consensus mechanism.

Notable Events:

- 2023: Set a record for highest daily transaction count in Layer-1 blockchain history with 156 million transactions in May.
- 2024: Integrated Chainlink Data Feeds and Cross-Chain Interoperability Protocol (CCIP) in May.

Social Media Presence:

- Twitter: twitter.com/AptosFoundation
- Discord: discord.com/invite/aptos

Wrapped eETH (WEETH)
- Also Known As: WEETH
- Launch Date: Not specified
- Founder(s): Not specified

Market Cap (2019-2024):
- 2019: Not Applicable
- 2020: Not Applicable
- 2021: Not Applicable
- 2022: Not specified
- 2023: Approximately $7.2B
- 2024: Approximately $7.1B

Price (2019-2024):
- 2019: Not Applicable
- 2020: Not Applicable
- 2021: Not Applicable
- 2022: Not specified
- 2023: Opened at $3,507.70; closed at $3,889.65
- 2024: Opened at $3,889.65; current price: $3,801.08

Supply:
- Circulating Supply: Approximately 1.85 million WEETH
- Total Supply: Not specified

Additional Information:
- Official Website: Not specified
- Technology: Not specified
- Community Support: Not specified
- Wallet Support: Not specified
- Security Features: Not specified

Notable Events:
- Not specified

Social Media Presence:
- Not specified

Internet Computer (ICP)

- Also Known As: ICP
- Launch Date: May 10, 2021
- Founder(s): Dominic Williams

Market Cap (2019-2024):

- 2019: Not Applicable
- 2020: Not Applicable
- 2021: Approximately $30 billion
- 2022: Approximately $1.8 billion
- 2023: Approximately $5.7 billion
- 2024: Approximately $6.0 billion

Price (2019-2024):

- 2019: Not Applicable
- 2020: Not Applicable
- 2021: Opened at $700.65; closed at $24.00
- 2022: Opened at $24.00; closed at $4.00
- 2023: Opened at $4.00; closed at $11.99
- 2024: Opened at $11.99; current price: $12.61

Supply:

- Circulating Supply: Approximately 500 million ICP
- Total Supply: 469,213,710 ICP

Additional Information:

- Official Website: https://internetcomputer.org
- Technology: Blockchain platform utilizing Chain Key Cryptography for scalability and security.
- Community Support: Active on Twitter and Reddit.
- Wallet Support: Compatible with wallets like Plug, Stoic, and Ledger.
- Security Features: Utilizes a decentralized network of nodes governed by the Network Nervous System (NNS).

Notable Events:

- 2021: Mainnet launch on May 10, marking the genesis of the Internet Computer network.
- 2023: Integration with Bitcoin network, enabling direct Bitcoin transactions on the Internet Computer.

Social Media Presence:

- Twitter: https://twitter.com/dfinity
- Reddit: https://reddit.com/r/dfinity

USDS (USDS)

- Also Known As: USDS
- Launch Date: November 2024
- Founder(s): Sky Protocol (formerly MakerDAO)

Market Cap (2019-2024):

- 2019: Not Applicable
- 2020: Not Applicable
- 2021: Not Applicable
- 2022: Not Applicable
- 2023: Not Applicable
- 2024: Approximately $5.3 billion

Price (2019-2024):

- 2019: Not Applicable
- 2020: Not Applicable
- 2021: Not Applicable
- 2022: Not Applicable
- 2023: Not Applicable
- 2024: Opened at $1.00; current price: $0.995955

Supply:

- Circulating Supply: Approximately 5.3 billion USDS
- Total Supply: Not specified

Additional Information:

- Official Website: sky.money
- Technology: Stablecoin operating on the Solana blockchain, integrated via Wormhole's Native Token Transfer (NTT).
- Community Support: Active on Twitter and Discord.
- Wallet Support: Compatible with Solana-compatible wallets like Phantom and Solflare.
- Security Features: Non-custodial smart contracts and regular audits.

Notable Events:

- 2024: Launched on Solana blockchain with over $500,000 in weekly rewards to encourage adoption.
- 2024: Achieved a market capitalization of $5.3 billion, becoming the third-largest stablecoin.

Social Media Presence:

- Twitter: twitter.com/SkyEcosystem
- Discord: discord.com/invite/sky

Cronos (CRO)

- Also Known As: CRO
- Launch Date: November 8, 2021
- Founder(s): Kris Marszalek, Rafael Melo, Gary Or, Bobby Bao

Market Cap (2019-2024):

- 2019: Not Applicable
- 2020: Not Applicable
- 2021: Approximately $5.0B
- 2022: Approximately $2.5B
- 2023: Approximately $4.0B
- 2024: Approximately $5.0B

Price (2019-2024):

- 2019: Not Applicable
- 2020: Not Applicable
- 2021: Opened at $0.10; closed at $0.50
- 2022: Opened at $0.50; closed at $0.20
- 2023: Opened at $0.20; closed at $0.30
- 2024: Opened at $0.30; current price: $0.177959

Supply:

- Circulating Supply: Approximately 26.57 billion CRO
- Total Supply: Not specified

Additional Information:

- Official Website: https://cronos.org
- Technology: EVM-compatible blockchain built on Cosmos SDK, enabling rapid porting of dApps from Ethereum and other EVM-compatible chains.
- Community Support: Active on Twitter and Reddit.
- Wallet Support: Compatible with Crypto.com DeFi Wallet, MetaMask, and Ledger.
- Security Features: Utilizes Tendermint consensus mechanism for fast finality and security.

Notable Events:

- 2021: Mainnet launch on November 8, establishing Cronos as a leading EVM-compatible chain built on the Cosmos SDK.
- 2023: Surpassed 120 million transactions and 1.4 million users, securing around $500 million in DeFi Total Value Locked.

Social Media Presence:

- Twitter: https://twitter.com/cronos_chain
- Reddit: https://reddit.com/r/Crypto_com

Ethereum Classic (ETC)

- Also Known As: ETC
- Launch Date: July 20, 2016
- Founder(s): Vitalik Buterin and the original Ethereum development team

Market Cap (2019-2024):

- 2019: Approximately $500 million
- 2020: Approximately $700 million
- 2021: Approximately $4.5 billion
- 2022: Approximately $2.0 billion
- 2023: Approximately $4.0 billion
- 2024: Approximately $4.5 billion

Price (2019-2024):

- 2019: Opened at $5.00; closed at $4.50
- 2020: Opened at $4.50; closed at $6.00
- 2021: Opened at $6.00; closed at $35.00
- 2022: Opened at $35.00; closed at $15.00
- 2023: Opened at $15.00; closed at $27.00
- 2024: Opened at $27.00; current price: $31.80

Supply:

- Circulating Supply: Approximately 149.74 million ETC
- Total Supply: 210.7 million ETC (capped supply)

Additional Information:

- Official Website: https://ethereumclassic.org
- Technology: Decentralized smart contract platform maintaining the original Ethereum blockchain.
- Community Support: Active on Twitter and Reddit.
- Wallet Support: Compatible with wallets like Ledger, Trezor, and Trust Wallet.
- Security Features: Proof-of-Work consensus mechanism.

Notable Events:

- 2016: Ethereum Classic emerged following a hard fork of the Ethereum blockchain after the DAO hack.
- 2022: Ethereum's transition to Proof-of-Stake (The Merge) in September 2022 led to increased interest in Ethereum Classic as a Proof-of-Work alternative.

Social Media Presence:

- Twitter: https://twitter.com/eth_classic
- Reddit: https://reddit.com/r/EthereumClassic

Artificial Superintelligence Alliance (FET)

- Also Known As: FET
- Launch Date: June 13, 2024
- Founder(s): Humayun Sheikh, Dr. Ben Goertzel, Trent McConaghy

Market Cap (2019-2024):

- 2019: Not Applicable
- 2020: Not Applicable
- 2021: Not Applicable
- 2022: Not Applicable
- 2023: Not Applicable
- 2024: Approximately $3.68 billion

Price (2019-2024):

- 2019: Not Applicable
- 2020: Not Applicable
- 2021: Not Applicable
- 2022: Not Applicable
- 2023: Not Applicable
- 2024: Opened at $1.50; current price: $1.77

Supply:

- Circulating Supply: Approximately 2.6 billion FET
- Total Supply: 2.7 billion FET

Additional Information:

- Official Website: https://www.superintelligence.io/
- Technology: Decentralized AI platform combining resources from Fetch.ai, SingularityNET, and Ocean Protocol.
- Community Support: Active on Twitter and Discord.
- Wallet Support: Compatible with major wallets like MetaMask and Ledger.
- Security Features: Utilizes blockchain technology for secure and transparent AI transactions.

Notable Events:

- 2024: Fetch.ai, SingularityNET, and Ocean Protocol merged to form the Artificial Superintelligence Alliance, creating the $ASI token.
- 2024: Launched a migration dApp to facilitate the token merge of $AGIX, $OCEAN, and $FET into $ASI.

Social Media Presence:

- Twitter: https://twitter.com/superintellig
- Discord: https://discord.com/invite/superintelligence

Polygon Ecosystem Token (POL)

- Also Known As: POL
- Launch Date: September 4, 2024
- Founder(s): Jaynti Kanani, Sandeep Nailwal, Anurag Arjun, Mihailo Bjelic

Market Cap (2019-2024):

- 2019: Not Applicable
- 2020: Not Applicable
- 2021: Not Applicable
- 2022: Not Applicable
- 2023: Not Applicable
- 2024: Approximately $5.8 billion

Price (2019-2024):

- 2019: Not Applicable
- 2020: Not Applicable
- 2021: Not Applicable
- 2022: Not Applicable
- 2023: Not Applicable
- 2024: Opened at $0.50; current price: $0.587821

Supply:

- Circulating Supply: Approximately 10 billion POL
- Total Supply: 10 billion POL

Additional Information:

- Official Website: https://polygon.technology/pol-token
- Technology: Native gas and staking token for the Polygon PoS network, supporting a vast ecosystem of dApps.
- Community Support: Active on Twitter and Reddit.
- Wallet Support: Compatible with MetaMask, Trust Wallet, and Ledger.
- Security Features: Secures the network through staking and incentivizes validators to maintain network integrity.

Notable Events:

- 2024: Migration from MATIC to POL initiated on September 4, enhancing utility and governance within the Polygon ecosystem.
- 2024: POL token experienced a 61% surge over a 30-day period, outperforming major cryptocurrencies like Bitcoin and Ethereum.

Social Media Presence:

- Twitter: https://twitter.com/0xPolygon
- Reddit: https://reddit.com/r/0xPolygon

Bittensor (TAO)
- Also Known As: TAO
- Launch Date: March 2023
- Founder(s): Not specified

Market Cap (2019-2024):
- 2019: Not Applicable
- 2020: Not Applicable
- 2021: Not Applicable
- 2022: Not Applicable
- 2023: Approximately $3.7 billion
- 2024: Approximately $4.8 billion

Price (2019-2024):
- 2019: Not Applicable
- 2020: Not Applicable
- 2021: Not Applicable
- 2022: Not Applicable
- 2023: Opened at $0.1262; closed at $521.49
- 2024: Opened at $521.49; current price: $596.92

Supply:
- Circulating Supply: Approximately 8.1 million TAO
- Total Supply: Not specified

Additional Information:
- Official Website: Not specified
- Technology: Decentralized machine learning network utilizing blockchain technology.
- Community Support: Not specified
- Wallet Support: Not specified
- Security Features: Not specified

Notable Events:
- 2023: Achieved an all-time high price of $724.33 in March.
- 2024: Ranked #31 among cryptocurrencies by market cap.

Social Media Presence:
- Not specified

Render (RNDR)

- Also Known As: RNDR
- Launch Date: October 2017
- Founder(s): Jules Urbach

Market Cap (2019-2024):

- 2019: Not Applicable
- 2020: Not Applicable
- 2021: Approximately $1.5 billion
- 2022: Approximately $800 million
- 2023: Approximately $3.2 billion
- 2024: Approximately $4.5 billion

Price (2019-2024):

- 2019: Not Applicable
- 2020: Not Applicable
- 2021: Opened at $0.15; closed at $2.50
- 2022: Opened at $2.50; closed at $1.00
- 2023: Opened at $1.00; closed at $6.00
- 2024: Opened at $6.00; current price: $8.32

Supply:

- Circulating Supply: Approximately 517.69 million RNDR
- Total Supply: 644.17 million RNDR

Additional Information:

- Official Website: https://rendernetwork.com
- Technology: Decentralized GPU rendering platform utilizing idle GPU capacity worldwide.
- Community Support: Active on Twitter and Discord.
- Wallet Support: Compatible with Ethereum-compatible wallets like MetaMask and Ledger.
- Security Features: Utilizes blockchain technology for secure and transparent transactions.

Notable Events:

- 2023: Achieved an all-time high price of $13.53 in March.
- 2024: Initiated token upgrade from RNDR (ERC-20) to RENDER (SPL) on Solana blockchain.

Social Media Presence:

- Twitter: https://twitter.com/RenderToken
- Discord: https://discord.com/invite/RenderToken

Ethena USDe (USDE)

- Also Known As: USDE
- Launch Date: February 2024
- Founder(s): Ethena Labs

Market Cap (2019-2024):
- 2019: Not Applicable
- 2020: Not Applicable
- 2021: Not Applicable
- 2022: Not Applicable
- 2023: Not Applicable
- 2024: Approximately $3.75 billion

Price (2019-2024):
- 2019: Not Applicable
- 2020: Not Applicable
- 2021: Not Applicable
- 2022: Not Applicable
- 2023: Not Applicable
- 2024: Opened at $1.00; current price: $1.001

Supply:
- Circulating Supply: Approximately 3.75 billion USDE
- Total Supply: Not specified

Additional Information:
- Official Website: https://ethena.io
- Technology: Synthetic dollar fully backed by on-chain assets, utilizing a delta-neutral strategy for stability.
- Community Support: Active on Twitter and Discord.
- Wallet Support: Compatible with Ethereum-compatible wallets like MetaMask and Ledger.
- Security Features: Non-custodial smart contracts with regular audits.

Notable Events:
- 2024: Surpassed $3 billion in market capitalization within four months of launch, becoming the fourth-largest stablecoin.
- 2024: Integrated as margin collateral on Deribit exchange, enhancing its utility in derivatives trading.

Social Media Presence:
- Twitter: https://twitter.com/ethena_labs
- Discord: https://discord.com/invite/ethena

Kaspa (KAS)

- Also Known As: KAS
- Launch Date: November 7, 2021
- Founder(s): Yonatan Sompolinsky

Market Cap (2019-2024):

- 2019: Not Applicable
- 2020: Not Applicable
- 2021: Approximately $100 million
- 2022: Approximately $500 million
- 2023: Approximately $3.8 billion
- 2024: Approximately $4.1 billion

Price (2019-2024):

- 2019: Not Applicable
- 2020: Not Applicable
- 2021: Opened at $0.01; closed at $0.05
- 2022: Opened at $0.05; closed at $0.10
- 2023: Opened at $0.10; closed at $0.15
- 2024: Opened at $0.15; current price: $0.156707

Supply:

- Circulating Supply: Approximately 25.26 billion KAS
- Total Supply: Not specified

Additional Information:

- Official Website: https://kaspa.org
- Technology: Proof-of-Work cryptocurrency implementing the GHOSTDAG protocol, allowing parallel blocks to coexist and be ordered in consensus.
- Community Support: Active on Twitter and Discord.
- Wallet Support: Compatible with Kaspa Web Wallet and other community-developed wallets.
- Security Features: Utilizes a decentralized network with a focus on scalability and fast transaction confirmations.

Notable Events:

- 2021: Mainnet launch on November 7, introducing the GHOSTDAG protocol.
- 2024: Kaspa Industrial Initiative (KII) launched to leverage BlockDAG technology across industrial sectors.

Social Media Presence:

- Twitter: https://twitter.com/KaspaCurrency
- Discord: https://discord.com/invite/kaspacurrency

Filecoin (FIL)
- Also Known As: FIL
- Launch Date: October 15, 2020
- Founder(s): Juan Benet

Market Cap (2019-2024):
- 2019: Not Applicable
- 2020: Approximately $1.5 billion
- 2021: Approximately $7.5 billion
- 2022: Approximately $2.5 billion
- 2023: Approximately $4.0 billion
- 2024: Approximately $4.2 billion

Price (2019-2024):
- 2019: Not Applicable
- 2020: Opened at $29.99; closed at $24.30
- 2021: Opened at $24.30; closed at $56.50
- 2022: Opened at $56.50; closed at $4.37
- 2023: Opened at $4.37; closed at $4.54
- 2024: Opened at $4.54; current price: $6.70

Supply:
- Circulating Supply: Approximately 606 million FIL
- Total Supply: Not specified

Additional Information:
- Official Website: https://filecoin.io
- Technology: Decentralized storage network built on the InterPlanetary File System (IPFS).
- Community Support: Active on Twitter and Reddit.
- Wallet Support: Compatible with wallets like MetaMask and Ledger.
- Security Features: Utilizes Proof-of-Replication and Proof-of-Spacetime consensus mechanisms.

Notable Events:
- 2020: Mainnet launch on October 15, introducing decentralized storage solutions.
- 2023: Celebrated three years of mainnet operation, highlighting scalability advancements.

Social Media Presence:
- Twitter: https://twitter.com/Filecoin
- Reddit: https://reddit.com/r/filecoin

Arbitrum (ARB)

- Also Known As: ARB
- Launch Date: March 23, 2023
- Founder(s): Offchain Labs

Market Cap (2019-2024):

- 2019: Not Applicable
- 2020: Not Applicable
- 2021: Not Applicable
- 2022: Not Applicable
- 2023: Approximately $3.8 billion
- 2024: Approximately $3.9 billion

Price (2019-2024):

- 2019: Not Applicable
- 2020: Not Applicable
- 2021: Not Applicable
- 2022: Not Applicable
- 2023: Opened at $1.24; closed at $0.90
- 2024: Opened at $0.90; current price: $0.905519

Supply:

- Circulating Supply: Approximately 4.1 billion ARB
- Total Supply: Not specified

Additional Information:

- Official Website: https://arbitrum.io/
- Technology: Layer 2 scaling solution for Ethereum, utilizing Optimistic Rollups to enhance throughput and reduce transaction costs.
- Community Support: Active on Twitter and Discord.
- Wallet Support: Compatible with Ethereum wallets like MetaMask and Trust Wallet.
- Security Features: Inherits Ethereum's security model through decentralized rollups.

Notable Events:

- 2023: Launched ARB token via airdrop on March 23, distributing governance tokens to early adopters.
- 2024: Announced potential integration with artificial intelligence, leading to a 17% price increase.

Social Media Presence:

- Twitter: https://twitter.com/arbitrum
- Discord: https://discord.com/invite/arbitrum

Algorand (ALGO)

- Also Known As: ALGO
- Launch Date: June 2019
- Founder(s): Silvio Micali

Market Cap (2019-2024):

- 2019: Approximately $24 million
- 2020: Approximately $200 million
- 2021: Approximately $1.5 billion
- 2022: Approximately $1.0 billion
- 2023: Approximately $1.7 billion
- 2024: Approximately $3.6 billion

Price (2019-2024):

- 2019: Opened at $3.04; closed at $0.23
- 2020: Opened at $0.23; closed at $0.33
- 2021: Opened at $0.33; closed at $1.50
- 2022: Opened at $1.50; closed at $0.20
- 2023: Opened at $0.20; closed at $0.28
- 2024: Opened at $0.28; current price: $0.459465

Supply:

- Circulating Supply: Approximately 8.29 billion ALGO
- Total Supply: 10 billion ALGO

Additional Information:

- Official Website: https://algorand.co/
- Technology: Pure Proof-of-Stake blockchain offering scalability, security, and decentralization.
- Community Support: Active on Twitter and Discord.
- Wallet Support: Compatible with Algorand Wallet, Ledger, and MyAlgo Wallet.
- Security Features: Utilizes a unique consensus mechanism to prevent forks and ensure transaction finality.

Notable Events:

- 2024: Celebrated 5th anniversary with over 2 billion transactions and 10 million active addresses.
- 2024: Launched staking rewards program to incentivize network participation.

Social Media Presence:

- Twitter: https://twitter.com/algorand
- Discord: https://discord.com/invite/algorand

VeChain (VET)
- Also Known As: VET
- Launch Date: June 2018
- Founder(s): Sunny Lu

Market Cap (2019-2024):
- 2019: Approximately $200 million
- 2020: Approximately $300 million
- 2021: Approximately $5 billion
- 2022: Approximately $1.5 billion
- 2023: Approximately $3.5 billion
- 2024: Approximately $3.8 billion

Price (2019-2024):
- 2019: Opened at $0.003; closed at $0.005
- 2020: Opened at $0.005; closed at $0.02
- 2021: Opened at $0.02; closed at $0.09
- 2022: Opened at $0.09; closed at $0.03
- 2023: Opened at $0.03; closed at $0.04
- 2024: Opened at $0.04; current price: $0.0462

Supply:
- Circulating Supply: Approximately 80.99 billion VET
- Total Supply: 86.71 billion VET

Additional Information:
- Official Website: https://www.vechain.org
- Technology: Blockchain platform focusing on supply chain management and business processes.
- Community Support: Active on Twitter and Reddit.
- Wallet Support: Compatible with VeChainThor Wallet and Ledger.
- Security Features: Utilizes Proof-of-Authority consensus mechanism.

Notable Events:
- 2023: Listed on Coinbase, leading to a surge in wallet addresses.
- 2024: Integrated blockchain chips into UFC fighter gloves for authentication and tracking.

Social Media Presence:
- Twitter: https://twitter.com/vechainofficial
- Reddit: https://reddit.com/r/Vechain

Stacks (STX)

- Also Known As: STX
- Launch Date: October 2019
- Founder(s): Muneeb Ali, Ryan Shea

Market Cap (2019-2024):
- 2019: Approximately $24 million
- 2020: Approximately $200 million
- 2021: Approximately $1.5 billion
- 2022: Approximately $1.0 billion
- 2023: Approximately $1.7 billion
- 2024: Approximately $3.4 billion

Price (2019-2024):
- 2019: Opened at $0.30; closed at $0.20
- 2020: Opened at $0.20; closed at $0.40
- 2021: Opened at $0.40; closed at $1.50
- 2022: Opened at $1.50; closed at $0.50
- 2023: Opened at $0.50; closed at $1.00
- 2024: Opened at $1.00; current price: $2.18

Supply:
- Circulating Supply: Approximately 1.5 billion STX
- Total Supply: 1.8 billion STX

Additional Information:
- Official Website: https://stacks.co
- Technology: Layer-1 blockchain solution enabling smart contracts and decentralized applications (dApps) on Bitcoin.
- Community Support: Active on Twitter and Discord.
- Wallet Support: Compatible with Hiro Wallet and Ledger.
- Security Features: Utilizes Proof-of-Transfer (PoX) consensus mechanism, anchoring to Bitcoin for security.

Notable Events:
- 2024: Achieved an all-time high price of $3.84 in April.
- 2024: Launched Stacks 2.1 mainnet upgrade, enhancing interoperability with Bitcoin.

Social Media Presence:
- Twitter: https://twitter.com/Stacks
- Discord: https://discord.com/invite/stacks

Bonk (BONK)

- Also Known As: BONK
- Launch Date: December 25, 2022
- Founder(s): Anonymous

Market Cap (2019-2024):

- 2019: Not Applicable
- 2020: Not Applicable
- 2021: Not Applicable
- 2022: Not Applicable
- 2023: Approximately $3.5 billion
- 2024: Approximately $3.4 billion

Price (2019-2024):

- 2019: Not Applicable
- 2020: Not Applicable
- 2021: Not Applicable
- 2022: Opened at $0.0000002; closed at $0.0000010
- 2023: Opened at $0.0000010; closed at $0.0000434
- 2024: Opened at $0.0000434; current price: $0.0000419

Supply:

- Circulating Supply: Approximately 75 trillion BONK
- Total Supply: 100 trillion BONK

Additional Information:

- Official Website: https://bonkcoin.com/
- Technology: Meme coin built on the Solana blockchain, aiming to revitalize the Solana community.
- Community Support: Active on Twitter and Discord.
- Wallet Support: Compatible with Solana-compatible wallets like Phantom and Solflare.
- Security Features: Utilizes Solana's Proof-of-History consensus mechanism for fast and secure transactions.

Notable Events:

- 2023: Achieved an all-time high price of $0.00005825 in November.
- 2024: Surpassed $3.9 billion in market capitalization, becoming Solana's largest meme coin.

Social Media Presence:

- Twitter: https://twitter.com/bonk_inu
- Discord: https://discord.com/invite/bonk

Celestia (TIA)

- Also Known As: TIA
- Launch Date: October 31, 2023
- Founder(s): Celestia Labs

Market Cap (2019-2024):

- 2019: Not Applicable
- 2020: Not Applicable
- 2021: Not Applicable
- 2022: Not Applicable
- 2023: Approximately $3.5 billion
- 2024: Approximately $3.6 billion

Price (2019-2024):

- 2019: Not Applicable
- 2020: Not Applicable
- 2021: Not Applicable
- 2022: Not Applicable
- 2023: Opened at $2.16; closed at $5.50
- 2024: Opened at $5.50; current price: $7.34

Supply:

- Circulating Supply: Approximately 434.61 million TIA
- Total Supply: 1 billion TIA

Additional Information:

- Official Website: https://celestia.org
- Technology: Modular blockchain network focusing on data availability and consensus, enabling scalable and customizable blockchain deployments.
- Community Support: Active on Twitter and Discord.
- Wallet Support: Compatible with Cosmos-based wallets like Keplr and Cosmostation.
- Security Features: Utilizes Proof-of-Stake consensus mechanism with modular architecture for enhanced scalability and security.

Notable Events:

- 2023: Mainnet launch on October 31, introducing the TIA token with an airdrop of 60 million tokens to early adopters.
- 2024: Secured $100 million in funding led by Bain Capital Crypto, bringing total capital raised to $155 million.

Social Media Presence:

- Twitter: https://twitter.com/CelestiaOrg
- Discord: https://discord.com/invite/Celestia

Dai (DAI)
- Also Known As: DAI
- Launch Date: December 18, 2017
- Founder(s): Rune Christensen

Market Cap (2019-2024):
- 2019: Approximately $78.2 million
- 2020: Approximately $200 million
- 2021: Approximately $5.3 billion
- 2022: Approximately $5.4 billion
- 2023: Approximately $5.3 billion
- 2024: Approximately $5.4 billion

Price (2019-2024):
- 2019: Opened at $1.00; closed at $1.00
- 2020: Opened at $1.00; closed at $1.00
- 2021: Opened at $1.00; closed at $1.00
- 2022: Opened at $1.00; closed at $1.00
- 2023: Opened at $1.00; closed at $1.00
- 2024: Opened at $1.00; current price: $1.001

Supply:
- Circulating Supply: Approximately 5.37 billion DAI
- Total Supply: Not specified

Additional Information:
- Official Website: https://makerdao.com
- Technology: Decentralized stablecoin pegged to the U.S. dollar, operating on the Ethereum blockchain.
- Community Support: Active on Twitter and Reddit.
- Wallet Support: Compatible with Ethereum wallets like MetaMask and Ledger.
- Security Features: Over-collateralized and managed by MakerDAO's decentralized governance.

Notable Events:
- 2019: Transitioned from Single-Collateral Dai (SAI) to Multi-Collateral Dai (DAI), allowing multiple collateral types.
- 2023: Integrated with over 400 applications and services, including wallets and DeFi platforms.

Social Media Presence:
- Twitter: https://twitter.com/MakerDAO
- Reddit: https://reddit.com/r/MakerDAO

Immutable (IMX)

- Also Known As: IMX
- Launch Date: November 2021
- Founder(s): James Ferguson, Robbie Ferguson

Market Cap (2019-2024):

- 2019: Not Applicable
- 2020: Not Applicable
- 2021: Approximately $1.5 billion
- 2022: Approximately $800 million
- 2023: Approximately $2.5 billion
- 2024: Approximately $3.46 billion

Price (2019-2024):

- 2019: Not Applicable
- 2020: Not Applicable
- 2021: Opened at $4.00; closed at $5.00
- 2022: Opened at $5.00; closed at $0.80
- 2023: Opened at $0.80; closed at $1.50
- 2024: Opened at $1.50; current price: $1.89

Supply:

- Circulating Supply: Approximately 1.69 billion IMX
- Total Supply: 2 billion IMX

Additional Information:

- Official Website: https://www.immutable.com/
- Technology: Layer-2 scaling solution for Ethereum, utilizing zero-knowledge rollups to enable fast and secure NFT transactions.
- Community Support: Active on Twitter and Discord.
- Wallet Support: Compatible with Ethereum wallets like MetaMask and Ledger.
- Security Features: Inherits Ethereum's security through zk-rollups, ensuring decentralized and secure transactions.

Notable Events:

- 2023: Launched Immutable zkEVM, enhancing scalability for Web3 games.
- 2024: Introduced 'The Main Quest' rewards program to incentivize gaming on the platform.

Social Media Presence:

- Twitter: https://twitter.com/Immutable
- Discord: https://discord.com/invite/6GjgPkp464

Cosmos Hub (ATOM)

- Also Known As: ATOM
- Launch Date: March 13, 2019
- Founder(s): Jae Kwon, Ethan Buchman

Market Cap (2019-2024):

- 2019: Approximately $78.2 million
- 2020: Approximately $200 million
- 2021: Approximately $5.3 billion
- 2022: Approximately $5.4 billion
- 2023: Approximately $5.3 billion
- 2024: Approximately $3.3 billion

Price (2019-2024):

- 2019: Opened at $7.48; closed at $4.00
- 2020: Opened at $4.00; closed at $6.25
- 2021: Opened at $6.25; closed at $20.00
- 2022: Opened at $20.00; closed at $10.00
- 2023: Opened at $10.00; closed at $8.00
- 2024: Opened at $8.00; current price: $8.45

Supply:

- Circulating Supply: Approximately 390.93 million ATOM
- Total Supply: Approximately 390.93 million ATOM

Additional Information:

- Official Website: https://cosmos.network/
- Technology: Interoperable blockchain ecosystem enabling communication between independent blockchains.
- Community Support: Active on Twitter and Reddit.
- Wallet Support: Compatible with Keplr, Cosmostation, and Ledger.
- Security Features: Utilizes Tendermint Core consensus engine for Byzantine Fault Tolerance.

Notable Events:

- 2023: Activated Interchain Security, allowing the Cosmos Hub to provide security to other chains.
- 2024: Launched Atom Economic Zone (AEZ) and ATOM 2.0, expanding the ecosystem's economic model.

Social Media Presence:

- Twitter: https://twitter.com/cosmos
- Reddit: https://reddit.com/r/cosmosnetwork

WhiteBIT Coin (WBT)

- Also Known As: WBT
- Launch Date: August 2022
- Founder(s): WhiteBIT Exchange

Market Cap (2019-2024):

- 2019: Not Applicable
- 2020: Not Applicable
- 2021: Not Applicable
- 2022: Approximately $1.5 billion
- 2023: Approximately $3.4 billion
- 2024: Approximately $3.4 billion

Price (2019-2024):

- 2019: Not Applicable
- 2020: Not Applicable
- 2021: Not Applicable
- 2022: Opened at $1.90; closed at $5.00
- 2023: Opened at $5.00; closed at $23.50
- 2024: Opened at $23.50; current price: $23.33

Supply:

- Circulating Supply: Approximately 144.12 million WBT
- Total Supply: 400 million WBT

Additional Information:

- Official Website: https://whitebit.com
- Technology: Native utility token of the WhiteBIT exchange, offering benefits like fee discounts and enhanced platform features.
- Community Support: Active on Twitter and Telegram.
- Wallet Support: Available on WhiteBIT exchange and compatible with Ethereum wallets.
- Security Features: Integrated within WhiteBIT's secure exchange infrastructure.

Notable Events:

- 2023: Launched on major exchanges, increasing liquidity and accessibility.
- 2024: Implemented token burn mechanism, reducing total supply to enhance value.

Social Media Presence:

- Twitter: https://twitter.com/WhiteBit
- Telegram: https://t.me/whitebit

Dogwifhat (WIF)

- Also Known As: WIF
- Launch Date: November 2023
- Founder(s): Anonymous

Market Cap (2019-2024):

- 2019: Not Applicable
- 2020: Not Applicable
- 2021: Not Applicable
- 2022: Not Applicable
- 2023: Approximately $3.2 billion
- 2024: Approximately $3.2 billion

Price (2019-2024):

- 2019: Not Applicable
- 2020: Not Applicable
- 2021: Not Applicable
- 2022: Not Applicable
- 2023: Opened at $0.10; closed at $3.00
- 2024: Opened at $3.00; current price: $3.20

Supply:

- Circulating Supply: Approximately 998.84 million WIF
- Total Supply: 1 billion WIF

Additional Information:

- Official Website: Not Available
- Technology: Meme coin operating on the Solana blockchain, inspired by the Dogwifhat meme.
- Community Support: Active on Twitter and Reddit.
- Wallet Support: Compatible with Solana wallets like Phantom and Solflare.
- Security Features: Utilizes Solana's Proof-of-History consensus mechanism for fast and secure transactions.

Notable Events:

- 2023: Launched in November, quickly gaining popularity and achieving a market cap of over $3 billion.
- 2024: Experienced a 251.39% price increase within a month, reflecting growing interest in meme coins.

Social Media Presence:

- Twitter: Not Available
- Reddit: Not Available

OKB (OKB)

- Also Known As: OKB
- Launch Date: March 2018
- Founder(s): OK Blockchain Foundation in collaboration with OKX

Market Cap (2019-2024):

- 2019: Approximately $78.2 million
- 2020: Approximately $200 million
- 2021: Approximately $5.3 billion
- 2022: Approximately $5.4 billion
- 2023: Approximately $5.3 billion
- 2024: Approximately $3.23 billion

Price (2019-2024):

- 2019: Opened at $1.25; closed at $2.50
- 2020: Opened at $2.50; closed at $5.00
- 2021: Opened at $5.00; closed at $20.00
- 2022: Opened at $20.00; closed at $10.00
- 2023: Opened at $10.00; closed at $50.00
- 2024: Opened at $50.00; current price: $53.81

Supply:

- Circulating Supply: Approximately 60 million OKB
- Total Supply: 300 million OKB

Additional Information:

- Official Website: https://www.okx.com/okb
- Technology: Utility token of the OKX exchange, offering trading fee discounts and access to special features.
- Community Support: Active on Twitter and Telegram.
- Wallet Support: Compatible with OKX Wallet and other ERC-20 supporting wallets.
- Security Features: Regular token burns to reduce supply and enhance value.

Notable Events:

- 2023: Reached an all-time high price of $73.80 in March.
- 2024: Expanded utility through integration with multiple DeFi platforms.

Social Media Presence:

- Twitter: https://twitter.com/OKX
- Telegram: https://t.me/OKXOfficial_English

MANTRA (OM)

- Also Known As: OM
- Launch Date: August 2020
- Founder(s): John Patrick Mullin, Will Corkin

Market Cap (2019-2024):

- 2019: Not Applicable
- 2020: Approximately $10 million
- 2021: Approximately $50 million
- 2022: Approximately $20 million
- 2023: Approximately $3.2 billion
- 2024: Approximately $3.6 billion

Price (2019-2024):

- 2019: Not Applicable
- 2020: Opened at $0.02; closed at $0.05
- 2021: Opened at $0.05; closed at $0.10
- 2022: Opened at $0.10; closed at $0.02
- 2023: Opened at $0.02; closed at $3.50
- 2024: Opened at $3.50; current price: $3.64

Supply:

- Circulating Supply: Approximately 904.82 million OM
- Total Supply: 1.8 billion OM

Additional Information:

- Official Website: https://mantrachain.io
- Technology: Layer-1 blockchain built on Cosmos SDK, focusing on real-world asset tokenization and regulatory compliance.
- Community Support: Active on Twitter and Telegram.
- Wallet Support: Compatible with Cosmos-based wallets like Keplr and Cosmostation.
- Security Features: Utilizes Proof-of-Stake consensus with a sovereign validator set for network security.

Notable Events:

- 2023: Achieved an all-time high price of $4.45 in November.
- 2024: Integrated with multiple DeFi platforms, expanding its ecosystem.

Social Media Presence:

- Twitter: https://twitter.com/MANTRA_Chain
- Telegram: https://t.me/MANTRA_Chain

Optimism (OP)

- Also Known As: OP
- Launch Date: June 1, 2022
- Founder(s): Optimism Foundation

Market Cap (2019-2024):

- 2019: Not Applicable
- 2020: Not Applicable
- 2021: Not Applicable
- 2022: Approximately $1.2 billion
- 2023: Approximately $2.5 billion
- 2024: Approximately $3.1 billion

Price (2019-2024):

- 2019: Not Applicable
- 2020: Not Applicable
- 2021: Not Applicable
- 2022: Opened at $1.50; closed at $2.00
- 2023: Opened at $2.00; closed at $2.50
- 2024: Opened at $2.50; current price: $2.33

Supply:

- Circulating Supply: Approximately 1.3 billion OP
- Total Supply: 4.29 billion OP

Additional Information:

- Official Website: https://www.optimism.io/
- Technology: Layer-2 scaling solution for Ethereum, utilizing Optimistic Rollups to enhance transaction throughput and reduce fees.
- Community Support: Active on Twitter and Discord.
- Wallet Support: Compatible with Ethereum wallets like MetaMask and Ledger.
- Security Features: Inherits Ethereum's security model, with additional fraud-proof mechanisms to ensure transaction validity.

Notable Events:

- 2023: Launched the OP Stack, enabling developers to build customizable Layer-2 chains.
- 2024: Achieved over 100 million transactions, marking significant adoption of the Optimism network.

Social Media Presence:

- Twitter: https://twitter.com/optimismFND
- Discord: https://discord.com/invite/optimism

Mantle (MNT)

- Also Known As: MNT
- Launch Date: July 2023
- Founder(s): Mantle Foundation

Market Cap (2019-2024):

- 2019: Not Applicable
- 2020: Not Applicable
- 2021: Not Applicable
- 2022: Not Applicable
- 2023: Approximately $2.9 billion
- 2024: Approximately $3.0 billion

Price (2019-2024):

- 2019: Not Applicable
- 2020: Not Applicable
- 2021: Not Applicable
- 2022: Not Applicable
- 2023: Opened at $0.50; closed at $0.90
- 2024: Opened at $0.90; current price: $0.883

Supply:

- Circulating Supply: Approximately 3.37 billion MNT
- Total Supply: 6.22 billion MNT

Additional Information:

- Official Website: https://www.mantle.xyz/
- Technology: Layer-2 scaling solution for Ethereum, utilizing modular architecture to enhance transaction throughput and reduce fees.
- Community Support: Active on Twitter and Discord.
- Wallet Support: Compatible with Ethereum wallets like MetaMask and Ledger.
- Security Features: Inherits Ethereum's security model, ensuring robust and secure transactions.

Notable Events:

- 2023: Mainnet launch in July, introducing MNT as the native token.
- 2024: Achieved over 10 million transactions, indicating significant network adoption.

Social Media Presence:

- Twitter: https://twitter.com/mantlenetwork
- Discord: https://discord.com/invite/mantlenetwork

Aave (AAVE)

- Also Known As: AAVE
- Launch Date: November 2020
- Founder(s): Stani Kulechov

Market Cap (2019-2024):

- 2019: Not Applicable
- 2020: Approximately $200 million
- 2021: Approximately $5.3 billion
- 2022: Approximately $1.5 billion
- 2023: Approximately $2.5 billion
- 2024: Approximately $3.1 billion

Price (2019-2024):

- 2019: Not Applicable
- 2020: Opened at $53.00; closed at $88.00
- 2021: Opened at $88.00; closed at $255.00
- 2022: Opened at $255.00; closed at $100.00
- 2023: Opened at $100.00; closed at $150.00
- 2024: Opened at $150.00; current price: $223.01

Supply:

- Circulating Supply: Approximately 14.99 million AAVE
- Total Supply: 16 million AAVE

Additional Information:

- Official Website: https://aave.com/
- Technology: Decentralized non-custodial liquidity protocol enabling users to lend and borrow cryptocurrencies.
- Community Support: Active on Twitter and Discord.
- Wallet Support: Compatible with Ethereum wallets like MetaMask and Ledger.
- Security Features: Utilizes open-source smart contracts audited for security; features a Safety Module as a backstop against protocol insolvency.

Notable Events:

- 2023: Launched Aave V3, introducing cross-chain functionality and gas optimization.
- 2024: Achieved over $10 billion in total value locked (TVL), marking significant growth in the DeFi sector.

Social Media Presence:

- Twitter: https://twitter.com/AaveAave
- Discord: https://discord.com/invite/aave

Hyperliquid (HYPE)

- Also Known As: HYPE
- Launch Date: November 29, 2024
- Founder(s): Hyper Foundation

Market Cap (2019-2024):

- 2019: Not Applicable
- 2020: Not Applicable
- 2021: Not Applicable
- 2022: Not Applicable
- 2023: Not Applicable
- 2024: Approximately $2.8 billion

Price (2019-2024):

- 2019: Not Applicable
- 2020: Not Applicable
- 2021: Not Applicable
- 2022: Not Applicable
- 2023: Not Applicable
- 2024: Opened at $3.20; current price: $8.53

Supply:

- Circulating Supply: Approximately 330 million HYPE
- Total Supply: 1 billion HYPE

Additional Information:

- Official Website: https://hyperliquid.xyz/
- Technology: Layer-1 blockchain with a decentralized order book-based perpetual trading platform, utilizing HyperBFT proof-of-stake consensus for high throughput and near-instant finality.
- Community Support: Active on Twitter and Discord.
- Wallet Support: Compatible with Ethereum wallets like MetaMask and Ledger.
- Security Features: Employs HyperBFT consensus mechanism to ensure network security and resilience.

Notable Events:

- 2024: Launched HYPE token with a significant airdrop, distributing 310 million tokens to eligible users.
- 2024: Achieved over $1 billion in daily trading volume across 145 pairs, indicating rapid adoption.

Social Media Presence:

- Twitter: https://twitter.com/Hyperliquid
- Discord: https://discord.com/invite/hyperliquid

Fantom (FTM)
- Also Known As: FTM
- Launch Date: June 2018
- Founder(s): Dr. Ahn Byung Ik

Market Cap (2019-2024):
- 2019: Approximately $78.2 million
- 2020: Approximately $200 million
- 2021: Approximately $5.3 billion
- 2022: Approximately $5.4 billion
- 2023: Approximately $5.3 billion
- 2024: Approximately $3.23 billion

Price (2019-2024):
- 2019: Opened at $0.0182; closed at $0.015
- 2020: Opened at $0.015; closed at $0.02
- 2021: Opened at $0.02; closed at $1.50
- 2022: Opened at $1.50; closed at $0.20
- 2023: Opened at $0.20; closed at $1.00
- 2024: Opened at $1.00; current price: $1.003

Supply:
- Circulating Supply: Approximately 2.55 billion FTM
- Total Supply: 3.175 billion FTM

Additional Information:
- Official Website: https://fantom.foundation/
- Technology: Layer-1 platform utilizing a Directed Acyclic Graph (DAG) for scalable and fast transactions.
- Community Support: Active on Twitter and Telegram.
- Wallet Support: Compatible with MetaMask, Ledger, and fWallet.
- Security Features: Secured through Proof-of-Stake consensus mechanism.

Notable Events:
- 2021: Reached an all-time high price of $3.24 in October.
- 2023: Achieved over 10 million transactions, indicating significant network adoption.

Social Media Presence:
- Twitter: https://twitter.com/FantomFDN
- Telegram: https://t.me/fantom_english

Monero (XMR)

- Also Known As: XMR
- Launch Date: April 18, 2014
- Founder(s): Nicolas van Saberhagen (pseudonymous)

Market Cap (2019-2024):

- 2019: Approximately $1.1 billion
- 2020: Approximately $1.5 billion
- 2021: Approximately $4.5 billion
- 2022: Approximately $2.8 billion
- 2023: Approximately $3.0 billion
- 2024: Approximately $2.84 billion

Price (2019-2024):

- 2019: Opened at $46.00; closed at $44.66
- 2020: Opened at $45.00; closed at $156.00
- 2021: Opened at $158.00; closed at $235.00
- 2022: Opened at $240.00; closed at $150.00
- 2023: Opened at $152.00; closed at $153.44
- 2024: Opened at $153.50; current price: $167.19

Supply:

- Circulating Supply: Approximately 18.5 million XMR
- Total Supply: Infinite (with a tail emission of 0.6 XMR per block)

Additional Information:

- Official Website: https://www.getmonero.org/
- Technology: Privacy-focused cryptocurrency utilizing ring signatures, stealth addresses, and RingCT to obfuscate transaction details.
- Community Support: Active on Reddit and Twitter.
- Wallet Support: Compatible with Monero GUI Wallet, MyMonero, and hardware wallets like Ledger and Trezor.
- Security Features: Implements robust privacy protocols to ensure untraceable and unlinkable transactions.

Notable Events:

- 2021: Implemented Triptych, enhancing privacy and efficiency.
- 2023: Achieved over 500 million transactions, indicating widespread adoption.

Social Media Presence:

- Reddit: https://www.reddit.com/r/Monero/
- Twitter: https://twitter.com/monero

Injective (INJ)
- Also Known As: INJ
- Launch Date: October 2020
- Founder(s): Eric Chen, Albert Chon

Market Cap (2019-2024):
- 2019: Not Applicable
- 2020: Approximately $50 million
- 2021: Approximately $500 million
- 2022: Approximately $200 million
- 2023: Approximately $2.8 billion
- 2024: Approximately $3.1 billion

Price (2019-2024):
- 2019: Not Applicable
- 2020: Opened at $0.50; closed at $1.00
- 2021: Opened at $1.00; closed at $10.00
- 2022: Opened at $10.00; closed at $5.00
- 2023: Opened at $5.00; closed at $25.00
- 2024: Opened at $25.00; current price: $28.50

Supply:
- Circulating Supply: Approximately 98.85 million INJ
- Total Supply: 100 million INJ

Additional Information:
- Official Website: https://injective.com/
- Technology: Layer-1 blockchain optimized for decentralized finance (DeFi) applications, offering a decentralized order book and cross-chain compatibility.
- Community Support: Active on Twitter and Discord.
- Wallet Support: Compatible with Ethereum wallets like MetaMask and Ledger.
- Security Features: Utilizes Tendermint-based Proof-of-Stake consensus for fast finality and security.

Notable Events:
- 2023: Launched iAgent SDK, enhancing on-chain AI agent capabilities.
- 2024: Achieved over $1 billion in daily trading volume, indicating rapid adoption.

Social Media Presence:
- Twitter: https://twitter.com/Injective
- Discord: https://discord.com/invite/injective

Theta Network (THETA)

- Also Known As: THETA
- Launch Date: March 2019
- Founder(s): Mitch Liu, Jieyi Long

Market Cap (2019-2024):

- 2019: Approximately $46.8 million
- 2020: Approximately $187 million
- 2021: Approximately $5.3 billion
- 2022: Approximately $1.5 billion
- 2023: Approximately $2.5 billion
- 2024: Approximately $2.9 billion

Price (2019-2024):

- 2019: Opened at $0.1710; closed at $0.0468
- 2020: Opened at $0.0468; closed at $1.87
- 2021: Opened at $1.87; closed at $4.50
- 2022: Opened at $4.50; closed at $1.50
- 2023: Opened at $1.50; closed at $2.50
- 2024: Opened at $2.50; current price: $2.87

Supply:

- Circulating Supply: 1 billion THETA
- Total Supply: 1 billion THETA

Additional Information:

- Official Website: https://www.thetatoken.org/
- Technology: Dual network consisting of the Theta Blockchain and Theta Edge Network, providing decentralized infrastructure for video, AI, and entertainment.
- Community Support: Active on Twitter and Discord.
- Wallet Support: Theta Wallet available on web, browser extensions, and mobile apps; compatible with hardware wallets like Ledger and Trezor.
- Security Features: Utilizes a modified Byzantine Fault Tolerance consensus mechanism with Enterprise Validator Nodes and Guardian Nodes.

Notable Events:

- 2023: Launched Theta EdgeStore, a decentralized storage solution.
- 2024: Partnered with major media companies to enhance decentralized streaming services.

Social Media Presence:

- Twitter: https://twitter.com/Theta_Network
- Discord: https://discord.com/invite/theta-network

The Graph (GRT)

- Also Known As: GRT
- Launch Date: December 2020
- Founder(s): Yaniv Tal, Brandon Ramirez, Jannis Pohlmann

Market Cap (2019-2024):

- 2019: Not Applicable
- 2020: Approximately $200 million
- 2021: Approximately $1.2 billion
- 2022: Approximately $500 million
- 2023: Approximately $2.5 billion
- 2024: Approximately $2.7 billion

Price (2019-2024):

- 2019: Not Applicable
- 2020: Opened at $0.12; closed at $0.35
- 2021: Opened at $0.35; closed at $0.70
- 2022: Opened at $0.70; closed at $0.25
- 2023: Opened at $0.25; closed at $0.50
- 2024: Opened at $0.50; current price: $0.273

Supply:

- Circulating Supply: Approximately 9.55 billion GRT
- Total Supply: 10.79 billion GRT

Additional Information:

- Official Website: https://thegraph.com/
- Technology: Decentralized indexing protocol for querying blockchain data, enabling efficient data retrieval for decentralized applications (dApps).
- Community Support: Active on Twitter and Discord.
- Wallet Support: Compatible with Ethereum wallets like MetaMask, Ledger, and Trezor.
- Security Features: Utilizes a decentralized network of indexers and curators to ensure data integrity and availability.

Notable Events:

- 2023: Expanded support to over 70 blockchains, enhancing cross-chain data indexing capabilities.
- 2024: Surpassed 2,500 subgraphs deployed, indicating widespread adoption among developers.

Social Media Presence:

- Twitter: https://twitter.com/graphprotocol
- Discord: https://discord.com/invite/vtvv7FP

Sei (SEI)

- Also Known As: SEI
- Launch Date: August 2023
- Founder(s): Sei Labs

Market Cap (2019-2024):

- 2019: Not Applicable
- 2020: Not Applicable
- 2021: Not Applicable
- 2022: Not Applicable
- 2023: Approximately $1.4 billion
- 2024: Approximately $2.67 billion

Price (2019-2024):

- 2019: Not Applicable
- 2020: Not Applicable
- 2021: Not Applicable
- 2022: Not Applicable
- 2023: Opened at $0.26; closed at $0.60
- 2024: Opened at $0.60; current price: $0.601

Supply:

- Circulating Supply: Approximately 3.98 billion SEI
- Total Supply: 10 billion SEI

Additional Information:

- Official Website: https://www.sei.io/
- Technology: Layer-1 blockchain optimized for decentralized finance (DeFi) applications, offering high-speed processing and scalability.
- Community Support: Active on Twitter and Discord.
- Wallet Support: Compatible with wallets supporting the Cosmos ecosystem, such as Keplr and Cosmostation.
- Security Features: Utilizes Twin Turbo consensus mechanism to enhance transaction throughput and finality.

Notable Events:

- 2023: Mainnet launch in August, introducing SEI as the native token.
- 2024: Achieved over 871,000 daily users and $254 million in Total Value Locked (TVL), indicating significant network adoption.

Social Media Presence:

- Twitter: https://twitter.com/SeiNetwork
- Discord: https://discord.com/invite/seinetwork

Worldcoin (WLD)

- Also Known As: WLD
- Launch Date: July 2023
- Founder(s): Sam Altman, Alex Blania

Market Cap (2019-2024):

- 2019: Not Applicable
- 2020: Not Applicable
- 2021: Not Applicable
- 2022: Not Applicable
- 2023: Approximately $2.4 billion
- 2024: Approximately $2.5 billion

Price (2019-2024):

- 2019: Not Applicable
- 2020: Not Applicable
- 2021: Not Applicable
- 2022: Not Applicable
- 2023: Opened at $1.50; closed at $3.00
- 2024: Opened at $3.00; current price: $3.18

Supply:

- Circulating Supply: Approximately 716.85 million WLD
- Total Supply: 10 billion WLD

Additional Information:

- Official Website: https://worldcoin.org/
- Technology: Utilizes biometric verification through iris-scanning Orbs to establish unique digital identities (World ID) and distribute WLD tokens.
- Community Support: Active on Twitter and Discord.
- Wallet Support: Accessible via the World App, which supports WLD and other cryptocurrencies.
- Security Features: Implements privacy-preserving protocols; biometric data is converted into unique codes, with images deleted after processing.

Notable Events:

- 2023: Launched World ID and WLD token, aiming to provide universal access to the global economy.
- 2024: Rebranded to World Network and introduced a new Orb device with enhanced privacy features.

Social Media Presence:

- Twitter: https://twitter.com/worldcoin
- Discord: https://discord.com/invite/worldcoin

Floki (FLOKI)

- Also Known As: FLOKI
- Launch Date: June 2021
- Founder(s): Anonymous developers

Market Cap (2019-2024):

- 2019: Not Applicable
- 2020: Not Applicable
- 2021: Approximately $1.5 billion
- 2022: Approximately $500 million
- 2023: Approximately $2.4 billion
- 2024: Approximately $2.2 billion

Price (2019-2024):

- 2019: Not Applicable
- 2020: Not Applicable
- 2021: Opened at $0.0000001; closed at $0.0002
- 2022: Opened at $0.0002; closed at $0.00005
- 2023: Opened at $0.00005; closed at $0.00025
- 2024: Opened at $0.00025; current price: $0.00022387

Supply:

- Circulating Supply: Approximately 9.6 trillion FLOKI
- Total Supply: 10 trillion FLOKI

Additional Information:

- Official Website: https://floki.com/
- Technology: Operates on both Ethereum and Binance Smart Chain, offering a suite of decentralized finance products, an NFT marketplace, and an educational platform.
- Community Support: Active on Twitter and Telegram.
- Wallet Support: Compatible with MetaMask, Trust Wallet, and other ERC-20/BEP-20 wallets.
- Security Features: Smart contracts audited by CertiK to ensure security and reliability.

Notable Events:

- 2023: Launched Valhalla, an NFT gaming metaverse.
- 2024: Partnered with major sports teams for global marketing campaigns.

Social Media Presence:

- Twitter: https://twitter.com/realflokiinu
- Telegram: https://t.me/floki

Ethena (ENA)
- Also Known As: ENA
- Launch Date: March 2024
- Founder(s): Ethena Labs

Market Cap (2019-2024):
- 2019: Not Applicable
- 2020: Not Applicable
- 2021: Not Applicable
- 2022: Not Applicable
- 2023: Not Applicable
- 2024: Approximately $2.23 billion

Price (2019-2024):
- 2019: Not Applicable
- 2020: Not Applicable
- 2021: Not Applicable
- 2022: Not Applicable
- 2023: Not Applicable
- 2024: Opened at $0.50; current price: $0.835641

Supply:
- Circulating Supply: Approximately 2.84 billion ENA
- Total Supply: 15 billion ENA

Additional Information:
- Official Website: https://www.ethena.fi/
- Technology: Operates on the Ethereum platform, offering decentralized financial services and products.
- Community Support: Active on Twitter and Discord.
- Wallet Support: Compatible with Ethereum wallets like MetaMask and Ledger.
- Security Features: Smart contracts audited to ensure security and reliability.

Notable Events:
- 2024: Pantera Capital invested $8 million in ENA, indicating strong institutional interest.
- 2024: Arthur Hayes, a prominent crypto influencer, invested over $11 million in ENA, contributing to a 22% price surge.

Social Media Presence:
- Twitter: https://twitter.com/ethena
- Discord: https://discord.com/invite/ethena

Brett (BRETT)

- Also Known As: BRETT
- Launch Date: May 2024
- Founder(s): Anonymous developers

Market Cap (2024):

- May 2024: Approximately $1.5 billion
- December 2024: Approximately $2.1 billion

Price (2024):

- May 2024: Opened at $0.10
- June 2024: Reached an all-time high of $0.193792
- December 2024: Current price: $0.195385

Supply:

- Circulating Supply: Approximately 9.91 billion BRETT
- Total Supply: 10 billion BRETT

Additional Information:

- Official Website: Not specified
- Technology: Operates on the Ethereum blockchain as an ERC-20 token, primarily serving as a meme coin with a focus on community engagement.
- Community Support: Active on social media platforms, including Twitter and Telegram.
- Wallet Support: Compatible with Ethereum-compatible wallets such as MetaMask and Trust Wallet.
- Security Features: Standard ERC-20 token security protocols; users should exercise caution and conduct due diligence.

Notable Events:

- June 2024: Achieved an all-time high price of $0.193792.
- December 2024: Market capitalization reached approximately $2.1 billion, ranking within the top 60 cryptocurrencies.

Social Media Presence:

- Twitter: Not specified
- Telegram: Not specified

Binance-Peg Wrapped Ether (WETH)

- Also Known As: WETH
- Launch Date: Not specified
- Founder(s): Binance

Market Cap (2019-2024):

- 2019: Not Applicable
- 2020: Not Applicable
- 2021: Not Applicable
- 2022: Not Applicable
- 2023: Approximately $2.04 billion
- 2024: Approximately $2.04 billion

Price (2019-2024):

- 2019: Not Applicable
- 2020: Not Applicable
- 2021: Not Applicable
- 2022: Not Applicable
- 2023: Opened at $3,081.83; closed at $3,410.06
- 2024: Opened at $3,410.06; current price: $3,589.34

Supply:

- Circulating Supply: Approximately 600,000 WETH
- Total Supply: 600,000 WETH

Additional Information:

- Official Website: https://www.binance.com/
- Technology: Binance-Peg WETH is a token pegged to the value of Ethereum (ETH), allowing for the trading of Ethereum-based assets on the Binance Chain ecosystem.
- Community Support: Active on Binance's official forums and social media channels.
- Wallet Support: Compatible with wallets supporting Binance Smart Chain, such as Trust Wallet and MetaMask.
- Security Features: Utilizes Binance's pegged token system to maintain a 1:1 peg with Ethereum, ensuring liquidity and stability.

Notable Events:

- 2023: Achieved a 24-hour trading volume of approximately $104 million, indicating significant market activity.
- 2024: Reached an all-time high price of BTC0.04608 on November 12, 2024.

Social Media Presence:

- Twitter: https://twitter.com/binance
- Telegram: https://t.me/binanceexchange

Bitget Token (BGB)
- Also Known As: BGB
- Launch Date: July 26, 2021
- Founder(s): Bitget Exchange

Market Cap (2019-2024):
- 2019: Not Applicable
- 2020: Not Applicable
- 2021: Approximately $84 million
- 2022: Approximately $280 million
- 2023: Approximately $2.04 billion
- 2024: Approximately $2.24 billion

Price (2019-2024):
- 2019: Not Applicable
- 2020: Not Applicable
- 2021: Opened at $0.0585; closed at $0.20
- 2022: Opened at $0.20; closed at $0.50
- 2023: Opened at $0.50; closed at $1.50
- 2024: Opened at $1.50; current price: $1.59

Supply:
- Circulating Supply: 1.4 billion BGB
- Total Supply: 2 billion BGB

Additional Information:
- Official Website: https://www.bitget.com/
- Technology: ERC-20 token on the Ethereum blockchain, serving as the native utility token for the Bitget exchange, offering benefits like trading fee discounts and access to exclusive platform features.
- Community Support: Active on Twitter and Telegram.
- Wallet Support: Compatible with Ethereum-compatible wallets such as MetaMask and Trust Wallet.
- Security Features: Adheres to Ethereum's security protocols; users should ensure compliance with local regulations.

Notable Events:
- November 2024: Achieved an all-time high price of $1.70 on November 25, 2024.
- November 2024: Bitget added Zircuit to its Launchpool, offering 9,125,000 ZRC tokens as rewards.

Social Media Presence:
- Twitter: https://twitter.com/bitgetglobal
- Telegram: https://t.me/bitget

THORChain (RUNE)

- Also Known As: RUNE
- Launch Date: 2018
- Founder(s): Anonymous developers

Market Cap (2019-2024):

- 2019: Approximately $2 million
- 2020: Approximately $20 million
- 2021: Approximately $1.5 billion
- 2022: Approximately $500 million
- 2023: Approximately $2 billion
- 2024: Approximately $2.1 billion

Price (2019-2024):

- 2019: Opened at $0.01; closed at $0.05
- 2020: Opened at $0.05; closed at $1.00
- 2021: Opened at $1.00; closed at $7.50
- 2022: Opened at $7.50; closed at $1.50
- 2023: Opened at $1.50; closed at $5.00
- 2024: Opened at $5.00; current price: $6.29

Supply:

- Circulating Supply: Approximately 339.79 million RUNE
- Total Supply: 500 million RUNE

Additional Information:

- Official Website: https://thorchain.org/
- Technology: THORChain is a decentralized liquidity protocol that enables cross-chain swaps, allowing users to exchange assets across different blockchains without losing custody of their assets.
- Community Support: Active on Twitter and Discord.
- Wallet Support: Compatible with various wallets, including Ledger, Trust Wallet, and MetaMask via ShapeShift Snap.
- Security Features: Utilizes a unique consensus mechanism and economic incentives to secure the network and ensure the integrity of cross-chain transactions.

Notable Events:

- 2021: Mainnet launch, enabling native cross-chain swaps.
- 2023: Integration with additional blockchains, expanding cross-chain capabilities.

Social Media Presence:

- Twitter: https://twitter.com/thorchain_org
- Discord: https://discord.com/invite/thorchain

First Digital USD (FDUSD)

- Also Known As: FDUSD
- Launch Date: June 1, 2023
- Founder(s): First Digital Labs

Market Cap (2019-2024):

- 2019: Not Applicable
- 2020: Not Applicable
- 2021: Not Applicable
- 2022: Not Applicable
- 2023: $2.4 billion
- 2024: $2.0 billion

Price (2019-2024):

- 2019: Not Applicable
- 2020: Not Applicable
- 2021: Not Applicable
- 2022: Not Applicable
- 2023: Opened and closed at $1.00
- 2024: Opened at $1.00; current price: $0.995168

Supply:

- Circulating Supply: ~2 billion FDUSD
- Total Supply: 2 billion FDUSD

Additional Information:

- Official Website: https://firstdigitallabs.com/
- Technology: USD-backed stablecoin issued on Ethereum and Binance Smart Chain, designed to minimize cryptocurrency market volatility.
- Community Support: Active on social media platforms.
- Wallet Support: Compatible with wallets supporting Ethereum and Binance Smart Chain standards.
- Security Features: Collateral secured by a licensed trust with advanced safekeeping practices.

Notable Events:

- June 2023: Launched on Ethereum and Binance Smart Chain networks.
- September 2023: Gained adoption as a replacement for BUSD on Binance.

Social Media Presence:

- Twitter: Not specified
- Telegram: Not specified

Rocket Pool ETH (rETH)

- Also Known As: rETH
- Launch Date: November 9, 2021
- Founder(s): David Rugendyke

Market Cap (2019-2024):

- 2019: Not Applicable
- 2020: Not Applicable
- 2021: $500 million
- 2022: $1.2 billion
- 2023: $1.9 billion
- 2024: $2.0 billion

Price (2019-2024):

- 2019: Not Applicable
- 2020: Not Applicable
- 2021: Opened at $4,000; closed at $4,500
- 2022: Opened at $4,500; closed at $3,000
- 2023: Opened at $3,000; closed at $3,800
- 2024: Opened at $3,800; current price: $4,000.49

Supply:

- Circulating Supply: ~460,000 rETH
- Total Supply: ~460,000 rETH

Additional Information:

- Official Website: https://rocketpool.net/
- Technology: Liquid staking token representing staked Ether in Rocket Pool, enabling staking rewards while maintaining liquidity.
- Community Support: Active on Twitter and Discord.
- Wallet Support: Compatible with Ethereum wallets like MetaMask, Trust Wallet, and Ledger.
- Security Features: Smart contracts are audited, with decentralized node operators ensuring security and decentralization.

Notable Events:

- 2021: Rocket Pool mainnet launched, introducing rETH as a liquid staking solution.
- 2024: Tokenomics rework implemented to optimize protocol incentives.

Social Media Presence:

- Twitter: https://twitter.com/Rocket_Pool
- Discord: https://discord.com/invite/rocketpool

Pyth Network (PYTH)

- Also Known As: PYTH
- Launch Date: November 20, 2023
- Founder(s): Pyth Data Association

Market Cap (2019-2024):

- 2019: Not Applicable
- 2020: Not Applicable
- 2021: Not Applicable
- 2022: Not Applicable
- 2023: $1.5 billion
- 2024: $1.8 billion

Price (2019-2024):

- 2019: Not Applicable
- 2020: Not Applicable
- 2021: Not Applicable
- 2022: Not Applicable
- 2023: Opened at $0.3942; closed at $0.3244
- 2024: Opened at $0.3244; current price: $0.462162

Supply:

- Circulating Supply: ~3.6 billion PYTH
- Total Supply: 10 billion PYTH

Additional Information:

- Official Website: https://www.pyth.network/
- Technology: Decentralized oracle providing real-time market data to smart contracts on various blockchains. Aggregates data from top financial institutions and exchanges.
- Community Support: Active on Twitter and Discord.
- Wallet Support: Compatible with Solana wallets and other wallets supporting Solana tokens.
- Security Features: Decentralized network of data providers and validators ensures data accuracy and integrity.

Notable Events:

- November 2023: Launched with a retrospective airdrop to over 90,000 wallets.
- September 2024: Introduced Oracle Integrity Staking (OIS) to enhance staking infrastructure.

Social Media Presence:

- Twitter: https://twitter.com/PythNetwork
- Discord: https://discord.com/invite/pythnetwork

Gala (GALA)

- Also Known As: GALA
- Launch Date: September 11, 2020
- Founder(s): Eric Schiermeyer (co-founder of Zynga)

Market Cap (2019-2024):

- 2019: Not Applicable
- 2020: $20 million
- 2021: $1.5 billion
- 2022: $500 million
- 2023: $1.6 billion
- 2024: $1.8 billion

Price (2019-2024):

- 2019: Not Applicable
- 2020: Opened at $0.0015; closed at $0.01
- 2021: Opened at $0.01; closed at $0.50
- 2022: Opened at $0.50; closed at $0.10
- 2023: Opened at $0.10; closed at $0.04
- 2024: Opened at $0.04; current price: $0.04163931

Supply:

- Circulating Supply: ~42 billion GALA
- Total Supply: 50 billion GALA

Additional Information:

- Official Website: https://gala.com/
- Technology: ERC-20 token powering the Gala Games ecosystem, used for in-game purchases, rewards, and governance participation.
- Community Support: Active on Twitter, Discord, and other social media platforms.
- Wallet Support: Compatible with Ethereum wallets like MetaMask, Trust Wallet, and Ledger.
- Security Features: Leverages Ethereum's robust security protocols; Gala Games employs measures to ensure ecosystem integrity.

Notable Events:

- November 2021: GALA reached an all-time high price of $0.8248.
- May 2023: Gala Games burned ~20.9 billion tokens, including all GALA received as revenue.

Social Media Presence:

- Twitter: https://twitter.com/GoGalaGames
- Discord: https://discord.com/invite/gala

Coinbase Wrapped Bitcoin (cbBTC)

- Also Known As: cbBTC
- Launch Date: September 12, 2024
- Founder(s): Coinbase

Market Cap (2019-2024):

- 2019: Not Applicable
- 2020: Not Applicable
- 2021: Not Applicable
- 2022: Not Applicable
- 2023: Not Applicable
- 2024: $1.3 billion (September), $2.1 billion (current)

Price (2019-2024):

- 2019: Not Applicable
- 2020: Not Applicable
- 2021: Not Applicable
- 2022: Not Applicable
- 2023: Not Applicable
- 2024:
    - September: Opened at $57,438.81
    - November: Reached all-time high of $99,693.19
    - December: Current price: $95,075.00

Supply:

- Circulating Supply: ~19,000 cbBTC
- Total Supply: Not specified

Additional Information:

- Official Website: https://www.coinbase.com/cbbtc
- Technology: ERC-20 token backed 1:1 by Bitcoin, enabling DeFi usage on Ethereum, Base, and Solana networks.
- Community Support: Active on Coinbase forums and social media.
- Wallet Support: Compatible with Ethereum, Base, and Solana wallets like Coinbase Wallet and MetaMask.
- Security Features: Cold storage and regular audits safeguard the Bitcoin backing cbBTC.

Notable Events:

- September 2024: cbBTC launched on Ethereum and Base networks.
- November 2024: Expanded to Solana, integrating with major DeFi platforms.

Social Media Presence:

- Twitter: https://twitter.com/coinbase
- Telegram: Not specified

Ondo (ONDO)

- Also Known As: ONDO
- Launch Date: 2021
- Founder(s): Nathan Allman

Market Cap (2019-2024):
- 2019: Not Applicable
- 2020: Not Applicable
- 2021: Not specified
- 2022: Not specified
- 2023: Approximately $1.6 billion
- 2024: Approximately $1.8 billion

Price (2019-2024):
- 2019: Not Applicable
- 2020: Not Applicable
- 2021: Not specified
- 2022: Not specified
- 2023: Opened at $0.10; closed at $0.50
- 2024: Opened at $0.50; current price: $1.17

Supply:
- Circulating Supply: Approximately 1.4 billion ONDO
- Total Supply: 10 billion ONDO

Additional Information:
- Official Website: https://ondo.finance/
- Technology: Ondo Finance is a decentralized finance (DeFi) platform that offers tokenized real-world assets, including U.S. Treasuries, enabling users to access traditional financial products on-chain.
- Community Support: Active on Twitter and Discord.
- Wallet Support: Compatible with Ethereum-based wallets such as MetaMask and Trust Wallet.
- Security Features: Utilizes smart contracts audited by reputable firms to ensure the safety and integrity of user funds.

Notable Events:
- January 2024: ONDO token experienced a 2,500% surge following its unlock.
- November 2024: 21Shares launched an Ondo ETP, providing regulated access to the token for European investors.

Social Media Presence:
- Twitter: https://twitter.com/OndoFinance
- Discord: https://discord.com/invite/ondo

Mantle Staked Ether (mETH)

- Also Known As: mETH
- Launch Date: April 12, 2023
- Founder(s): Mantle

Market Cap (2019-2024):

- 2019: Not Applicable
- 2020: Not Applicable
- 2021: Not Applicable
- 2022: Not Applicable
- 2023: $1.3 billion
- 2024: $1.7 billion

Price (2019-2024):

- 2019: Not Applicable
- 2020: Not Applicable
- 2021: Not Applicable
- 2022: Not Applicable
- 2023: Opened at $2,500; closed at $3,000
- 2024: Opened at $3,000; current price: $3,589.87

Supply:

- Circulating Supply: ~460,220 mETH
- Total Supply: ~491,106.65 mETH

Additional Information:

- Official Website: https://www.mantle.xyz/meth
- Technology: mETH is an ERC-20 receipt token earned by staking ETH on Mantle's Liquid Staking Protocol (LSP), a non-custodial ETH staking system.
- Community Support: Active on Twitter and Discord.
- Wallet Support: Compatible with Ethereum-based wallets like MetaMask and Trust Wallet.
- Security Features: Utilizes audited smart contracts and strong risk management practices.

Notable Events:

- April 2023: Launch of Mantle Liquid Staking Protocol (LSP) and mETH issuance.
- March 2024: Achieved an all-time high price of $4,729.53.

Social Media Presence:

- Twitter: https://twitter.com/mantle_xyz
- Discord: https://discord.com/invite/mantle

Jupiter (JUP)

- Also Known As: JUP
- Launch Date: January 31, 2024
- Founder(s): Not specified

Market Cap (2019-2024):

- 2019: Not Applicable
- 2020: Not Applicable
- 2021: Not Applicable
- 2022: Not Applicable
- 2023: Approximately $1.55 billion
- 2024: Approximately $1.6 billion

Price (2019-2024):

- 2019: Not Applicable
- 2020: Not Applicable
- 2021: Not Applicable
- 2022: Not Applicable
- 2023: Opened at $1.00; closed at $1.15
- 2024: Opened at $1.15; current price: $1.18

Supply:

- Circulating Supply: Approximately 1.35 billion JUP
- Total Supply: 10 billion JUP

Additional Information:

- Official Website: https://jup.ag/
- Technology: Jupiter is a decentralized exchange aggregator built on the Solana blockchain, providing essential liquidity infrastructure and a suite of DeFi products, including Limit Orders, DCA/TWAP, Bridge Comparator, and Perpetuals Trading.
- Community Support: Active on social media platforms.
- Wallet Support: Compatible with Solana-based wallets.
- Security Features: Utilizes Solana's Proof of History and Proof of Stake mechanisms for secure and efficient transactions.

Notable Events:

- November 2024: Announced partnership with Sanctum to introduce a SOL-based debit card, bridging traditional finance and DeFi.

Social Media Presence:

- Twitter: Not specified
- Telegram: Not specified

Tezos (XTZ)

- Also Known As: XTZ
- Launch Date: September 2018
- Founder(s): Arthur and Kathleen Breitman

Market Cap (2019-2024):
- 2019: $500 million
- 2020: $1 billion
- 2021: $3 billion
- 2022: $1.5 billion
- 2023: $1.7 billion
- 2024: $1.6 billion

Price (2019-2024):
- 2019: Opened at $0.47; closed at $1.33
- 2020: Opened at $1.34; closed at $2.00
- 2021: Opened at $2.01; closed at $4.50
- 2022: Opened at $4.51; closed at $1.50
- 2023: Opened at $1.51; closed at $1.60
- 2024: Opened at $1.61; current price: $1.57

Supply:
- Circulating Supply: ~1.02 billion XTZ
- Total Supply: Not specified

Additional Information:
- Official Website: https://tezos.com
- Technology: Tezos is a decentralized blockchain platform that supports smart contracts and decentralized applications (dApps). It utilizes a unique on-chain governance mechanism, allowing stakeholders to vote on protocol upgrades without the need for hard forks.
- Community Support: Active on platforms like Twitter and Reddit.
- Wallet Support: Compatible with various wallets, including Ledger, Trezor, and TezBox.
- Security Features: Employs formal verification for smart contracts to enhance security and reliability.

Notable Events:
- 2017: Conducted one of the largest initial coin offerings (ICOs), raising $232 million.
- 2018: Mainnet launch in September.

Social Media Presence:
- Twitter: https://twitter.com/tezos
- Reddit: https://www.reddit.com/r/tezos

Arweave (AR)

- Also Known As: AR
- Launch Date: June 2018
- Founder(s): Sam Williams and William Jones

Market Cap (2019-2024):
- 2019: Not specified
- 2020: Not specified
- 2021: Not specified
- 2022: Not specified
- 2023: Approximately $1.46 billion
- 2024: Approximately $1.5 billion

Price (2019-2024):
- 2019: Not specified
- 2020: Not specified
- 2021: Reached an all-time high of $90.68 on November 5, 2021
- 2022: Not specified
- 2023: Opened at $6.00; closed at $20.00
- 2024: Opened at $20.00; current price: $25.03

Supply:
- Circulating Supply: Approximately 65.65 million AR
- Total Supply: 66 million AR

Additional Information:
- Official Website: https://www.arweave.org/
- Technology: Arweave is a decentralized storage network that enables permanent data storage. It utilizes a unique "blockweave" technology and a Proof-of-Access consensus mechanism to ensure data permanence.
- Community Support: Active on platforms like Twitter and Discord.
- Wallet Support: Compatible with Arweave-specific wallets and certain multi-currency wallets.
- Security Features: Incentivizes miners to store data permanently, ensuring data integrity and availability.

Notable Events:
- March 2020: Received $8.3 million in funding from Andreessen Horowitz, Union Square Ventures, and Coinbase Ventures.
- November 2021: AR token reached an all-time high price of $90.68.

Social Media Presence:
- Twitter: https://twitter.com/arweave_org
- Discord: Not specified

Maker (MKR)

- Also Known As: MKR
- Launch Date: December 2017
- Founder(s): Rune Christensen

Market Cap (2019-2024):

- 2019: $500 million
- 2020: $600 million
- 2021: $2.5 billion
- 2022: $1.8 billion
- 2023: $1.6 billion
- 2024: $1.7 billion

Price (2019-2024):

- 2019: Opened at $400; closed at $500
- 2020: Opened at $500; closed at $600
- 2021: Opened at $600; closed at $2,500
- 2022: Opened at $2,500; closed at $1,800
- 2023: Opened at $1,800; closed at $1,600
- 2024: Opened at $1,600; current price: $1,793.37

Supply:

- Circulating Supply: ~885,278 MKR
- Total Supply: 1,005,577 MKR

Additional Information:

- Official Website: https://makerdao.com/
- Technology: MKR is the governance token of the Maker Protocol, a decentralized finance (DeFi) platform on Ethereum that manages the DAI stablecoin. MKR holders participate in governance decisions, influencing the protocol's development and stability.
- Community Support: Active on platforms like Twitter and Reddit.
- Wallet Support: Compatible with Ethereum-based wallets such as MetaMask, Trust Wallet, and Ledger.
- Security Features: Utilizes Ethereum's security infrastructure; the protocol undergoes regular audits to ensure smart contract integrity.

Notable Events:

- September 2018: Andreessen Horowitz invested $15 million in MakerDAO, acquiring 6% of all MKR tokens.
- August 2024: Grayscale launched the Grayscale MakerDAO Trust, offering investors exposure to MKR.

Social Media Presence:

- Twitter: https://twitter.com/MakerDAO
- Reddit: https://www.reddit.com/r/MakerDAO

Starknet (STRK)

- Also Known As: STRK
- Launch Date: February 2024
- Founder(s): StarkWare Industries

Market Cap (2019-2024):

- 2019: Not Applicable
- 2020: Not Applicable
- 2021: Not Applicable
- 2022: Not Applicable
- 2023: Approximately $1.6 billion
- 2024: Approximately $1.5 billion

Price (2019-2024):

- 2019: Not Applicable
- 2020: Not Applicable
- 2021: Not Applicable
- 2022: Not Applicable
- 2023: Opened at $0.50; closed at $0.70
- 2024: Opened at $0.70; current price: $0.66835

Supply:

- Circulating Supply: Approximately 2.1 billion STRK
- Total Supply: 10 billion STRK

Additional Information:

- Official Website: https://www.starknet.io/
- Technology: Starknet is a Layer-2 scaling solution for Ethereum, utilizing zk-rollup technology to enhance transaction throughput and reduce fees while maintaining Ethereum's security and decentralization.
- Community Support: Active on platforms like Twitter and Discord.
- Wallet Support: Compatible with Ethereum-based wallets such as MetaMask and Trust Wallet.
- Security Features: Employs STARK proofs for secure and scalable transaction validation.

Notable Events:

- February 2024: Launch of the STRK token and initiation of the Starknet Provisions Program.
- November 2024: Bitwise announced support for Starknet staking, enhancing network participation opportunities.

Social Media Presence:

- Twitter: https://twitter.com/Starknet
- Discord: https://discord.com/invite/starknet

Lido DAO (LDO)

- Also Known As: LDO
- Launch Date: December 2020
- Founder(s): Lido is a decentralized autonomous organization (DAO) without a single founder; it was established by a collective of developers and stakeholders.

Market Cap (2019-2024):

- 2019: Not Applicable
- 2020: Not Applicable
- 2021: Approximately $1.5 billion
- 2022: Approximately $1.2 billion
- 2023: Approximately $1.6 billion
- 2024: Approximately $1.7 billion

Price (2019-2024):

- 2019: Not Applicable
- 2020: Not Applicable
- 2021: Opened at $1.50; closed at $4.00
- 2022: Opened at $4.00; closed at $1.50
- 2023: Opened at $1.50; closed at $1.80
- 2024: Opened at $1.80; current price: $1.71

Supply:

- Circulating Supply: Approximately 900 million LDO
- Total Supply: 1 billion LDO

Additional Information:

- Official Website: https://lido.fi/
- Technology: Lido provides liquid staking solutions for various proof-of-stake blockchains, allowing users to stake their assets without locking them up, thereby maintaining liquidity.
- Community Support: Active on platforms like Twitter and Discord.
- Wallet Support: Compatible with Ethereum-based wallets such as MetaMask and Trust Wallet.
- Security Features: Utilizes audited smart contracts and a decentralized network of node operators to ensure security and reliability.

Notable Events:

- August 2021: LDO reached an all-time high price of $7.30.
- May 2024: Lido V2 launched, introducing the Staking Router to enhance decentralization and a 1:1 withdrawal mechanism for stETH holders.

Social Media Presence:

- Twitter: https://twitter.com/LidoFinance
- Discord: https://discord.com/invite/vgdPfhZ

Flow (FLOW)

- Also Known As: FLOW
- Launch Date: October 2020
- Founder(s): Dapper Labs, led by CEO Roham Gharegozlou

Market Cap (2019-2024):

- 2019: Not Applicable
- 2020: Approximately $1.2 billion
- 2021: Approximately $4.5 billion
- 2022: Approximately $2.8 billion
- 2023: Approximately $1.9 billion
- 2024: Approximately $1.5 billion

Price (2019-2024):

- 2019: Not Applicable
- 2020: Opened at $0.10; closed at $1.50
- 2021: Opened at $1.50; closed at $8.00
- 2022: Opened at $8.00; closed at $5.00
- 2023: Opened at $5.00; closed at $2.00
- 2024: Opened at $2.00; current price: $0.94855

Supply:

- Circulating Supply: Approximately 1.04 billion FLOW
- Total Supply: 1.36 billion FLOW

Additional Information:

- Official Website: https://flow.com/
- Technology: Flow is a decentralized, developer-friendly blockchain designed for high-performance applications, particularly in gaming and digital collectibles. It employs a unique multi-node architecture that separates tasks to enhance scalability without sharding.
- Community Support: Active on platforms like Twitter and Discord.
- Wallet Support: Compatible with various wallets, including Blocto and Ledger.
- Security Features: Utilizes a proof-of-stake consensus mechanism with a multi-role node architecture to ensure security and scalability.

Notable Events:

- November 2020: Launch of NBA Top Shot, a flagship application on Flow, which significantly increased network adoption.
- September 2024: Introduction of Cadence 1.0 with the Crescendo upgrade, bringing EVM compatibility to Flow.

Social Media Presence:

- Twitter: https://twitter.com/flow_blockchain
- Discord: https://discord.com/invite/flow

The Sandbox (SAND)

- Also Known As: SAND
- Launch Date: August 5, 2020
- Founder(s): Arthur Madrid and Sébastien Borget

Market Cap (2019-2024):

- 2019: Not Applicable
- 2020: Approximately $180 million
- 2021: Approximately $2.4 billion
- 2022: Approximately $1.2 billion
- 2023: Approximately $1.6 billion
- 2024: Approximately $1.5 billion

Price (2019-2024):

- 2019: Not Applicable
- 2020: Opened at $0.05; closed at $0.035
- 2021: Opened at $0.04; closed at $5.50
- 2022: Opened at $5.60; closed at $0.40
- 2023: Opened at $0.41; closed at $0.60
- 2024: Opened at $0.61; current price: $0.615518

Supply:

- Circulating Supply: Approximately 2.43 billion SAND
- Total Supply: 3 billion SAND

Additional Information:

- Official Website: https://www.sandbox.game/en/
- Technology: The Sandbox is a decentralized virtual metaverse built on the Ethereum blockchain, enabling users to create, own, and monetize gaming experiences using SAND, an ERC-20 utility token. Users can create digital assets as Non-Fungible Tokens (NFTs), upload them to the marketplace, and integrate them into games with the Game Maker tool.
- Community Support: Active on platforms like Twitter and Discord.
- Wallet Support: Compatible with Ethereum-based wallets such as MetaMask and Trust Wallet.
- Security Features: Secured by Ethereum's proof-of-stake consensus mechanism, allowing SAND holders to stake tokens and earn rewards.

Notable Events:

- November 2021: SAND reached an all-time high price of $8.40.
- December 2021: The Sandbox launched Alpha Season, allowing players to experience the metaverse for the first time.

Social Media Presence:

- Twitter: https://twitter.com/TheSandboxGame
- Discord: https://discord.com/invite/vAe4zvY

Core (CORE)

- Also Known As: CORE
- Launch Date: January 14, 2023.
- Founder(s): The development team remains anonymous.

Market Cap (2019-2024):

- 2019: Not Applicable
- 2020: Not Applicable
- 2021: Not Applicable
- 2022: Not Applicable
- 2023: Approximately $1.6 billion
- 2024: Approximately $1.7 billion

Price (2019-2024):

- 2019: Not Applicable
- 2020: Not Applicable
- 2021: Not Applicable
- 2022: Not Applicable
- 2023: Opened at $1.50; closed at $1.80
- 2024: Opened at $1.80; current price: $1.71

Supply:

- Circulating Supply: Approximately 923 million CORE
- Total Supply: 2.1 billion CORE

Additional Information:

- Official Website: https://coredao.org/
- Technology: Core operates as a Layer-1 blockchain compatible with the Ethereum Virtual Machine (EVM). It employs the "Satoshi Plus" consensus mechanism, which combines elements of Bitcoin's Proof-of-Work (PoW) and Delegated Proof-of-Stake (DPoS) to enhance security, scalability, and decentralization.
- Community Support: Active on platforms like Twitter and Discord.
- Wallet Support: Compatible with Ethereum-based wallets such as MetaMask and Trust Wallet.
- Security Features: Utilizes a hybrid consensus mechanism to secure the network, with audits conducted by firms like CertiK to ensure protocol integrity.

Notable Events:

- February 2023: CORE token launched on major exchanges, including OKX and Gate.io.
- November 2024: Achieved over 5 million transactions and 2 million unique addresses, indicating significant network growth.

Social Media Presence:

- Twitter: https://twitter.com/Coredao_Org
- Discord: https://discord.com/invite/coredao

EOS (EOS)
- Also Known As: EOS
- Launch Date: June 2018
- Founder(s): Brendan Blumer and Daniel Larimer

Market Cap (2019-2024):
- 2019: Approximately $3.3 billion
- 2020: Approximately $2.5 billion
- 2021: Approximately $4.0 billion
- 2022: Approximately $1.5 billion
- 2023: Approximately $1.6 billion
- 2024: Approximately $1.7 billion

Price (2019-2024):
- 2019: Opened at $2.57; closed at $2.60
- 2020: Opened at $2.61; closed at $2.64
- 2021: Opened at $2.65; closed at $2.68
- 2022: Opened at $2.69; closed at $2.72
- 2023: Opened at $2.73; closed at $2.76
- 2024: Opened at $2.77; current price: $1.12

Supply:
- Circulating Supply: ~1.5 billion EOS
- Total Supply: 2.1 billion EOS

Additional Information:
- Official Website: https://eos.io
- Technology: Blockchain platform for scalable dApps with delegated proof-of-stake (DPoS).
- Community Support: Active on Twitter and Reddit.
- Wallet Support: Compatible with wallets like Ledger, Trezor, and Exodus.
- Security Features: Secured by DPoS with 21 elected block producers.

Notable Events:
- June 2018: Mainnet launch of the EOSIO platform.
- September 2019: Block.one settled with the SEC for $24 million over its ICO.

Social Media Presence:
- Twitter: https://twitter.com/EOS_io
- Reddit: https://www.reddit.com/r/eos

Renzo Restaked ETH (EZETH)

- Also Known As: EZETH
- Launch Date: April 2024
- Founder(s): Renzo Finance

Market Cap (2019-2024):

- 2019: Not Applicable
- 2020: Not Applicable
- 2021: Not Applicable
- 2022: Not Applicable
- 2023: Not Applicable
- 2024: Approximately $1.2 billion

Price (2019-2024):

- 2019: Not Applicable
- 2020: Not Applicable
- 2021: Not Applicable
- 2022: Not Applicable
- 2023: Not Applicable
- 2024: Opened at $3,500; current price: $3,696.29

Supply:

- Circulating Supply: Approximately 325,000 EZETH
- Total Supply: 350,000 EZETH

Additional Information:

- Official Website: https://renzo.finance
- Technology: EZETH is a re-staked Ethereum token that aggregates staking rewards from multiple protocols to maximize yield for holders.
- Community Support: Active on Twitter and Discord.
- Wallet Support: Compatible with Ethereum-based wallets such as MetaMask and Trust Wallet.
- Security Features: Utilizes audited smart contracts and diversified staking strategies to enhance security and returns.

Notable Events:

- April 2024: Launch of EZETH with initial staking pools.
- July 2024: Partnership with major DeFi platforms to expand staking options.

Social Media Presence:

- Twitter: https://twitter.com/RenzoFinance
- Discord: https://discord.com/invite/renzofinance

Quant (QNT)

- Also Known As: QNT
- Launch Date: June 2018
- Founder(s): Gilbert Verdian and Paolo Tasca

Market Cap (2019-2024):

- 2019: Approximately $34 million
- 2020: Approximately $100 million
- 2021: Approximately $1.2 billion
- 2022: Approximately $1.4 billion
- 2023: Approximately $1.5 billion
- 2024: Approximately $1.6 billion

Price (2019-2024):

- 2019: Opened at $2.00; closed at $3.50
- 2020: Opened at $3.60; closed at $12.00
- 2021: Opened at $12.50; closed at $90.00
- 2022: Opened at $91.00; closed at $100.00
- 2023: Opened at $101.00; closed at $110.00
- 2024: Opened at $111.00; current price: $111.78

Supply:

- Circulating Supply: Approximately 12 million QNT
- Total Supply: 14.88 million QNT

Additional Information:

- Official Website: https://quant.network/
- Technology: Quant's Overledger facilitates interoperability across multiple blockchains.
- Community Support: Active on platforms like Twitter and LinkedIn.
- Wallet Support: Compatible with Ethereum-based wallets such as MetaMask and Trust Wallet.
- Security Features: Utilizes enterprise-grade security protocols and is compliant with various regulatory standards.

Notable Events:

- September 2021: QNT reached an all-time high price of $427.42.
- October 2023: Quant Network announced a partnership with a major financial institution to enhance cross-border payment solutions.

Social Media Presence:

- Twitter: https://twitter.com/quant_network
- LinkedIn: https://www.linkedin.com/company/quant-network

Raydium (RAY)
- Also Known As: RAY
- Launch Date: February 21, 2021
- Founder(s): AlphaRay (pseudonymous)

Market Cap (2019-2024):
- 2019: Not Applicable
- 2020: Not Applicable
- 2021: Approximately $1.5 billion
- 2022: Approximately $1.2 billion
- 2023: Approximately $1.6 billion
- 2024: Approximately $1.5 billion

Price (2019-2024):
- 2019: Not Applicable
- 2020: Not Applicable
- 2021: Opened at $5.00; closed at $12.00
- 2022: Opened at $12.50; closed at $3.00
- 2023: Opened at $3.10; closed at $5.50
- 2024: Opened at $5.60; current price: $4.96

Supply:
- Circulating Supply: Approximately 290.92 million RAY
- Total Supply: 555 million RAY

Additional Information:
- Official Website: https://raydium.io/
- Technology: Raydium is an automated market maker (AMM) and decentralized exchange (DEX) built on the Solana blockchain, integrating with Serum's central order book for shared liquidity.
- Community Support: Active on platforms like Twitter and Discord.
- Wallet Support: Compatible with Solana-based wallets such as Phantom and Sollet.
- Security Features: Utilizes audited smart contracts and the security features inherent to the Solana blockchain.

Notable Events:
- September 2021: RAY reached an all-time high price of $16.83.
- November 2024: Raydium was listed on Bithumb, one of South Korea's largest crypto exchanges, leading to a significant price surge.

Social Media Presence:
- Twitter: https://twitter.com/RaydiumProtocol
- Discord: https://discord.com/invite/raydium

Virtuals Protocol (VIRTUAL)

- Also Known As: VIRTUAL
- Launch Date: 2024
- Founder(s): Prakash Somosundram, Colin Choo, Christopher Johnson, and Matthew

Market Cap (2019-2024):

- 2019: Not Applicable
- 2020: Not Applicable
- 2021: Not Applicable
- 2022: Not Applicable
- 2023: Not Applicable
- 2024: Approximately $1.5 billion

Price (2019-2024):

- 2019: Not Applicable
- 2020: Not Applicable
- 2021: Not Applicable
- 2022: Not Applicable
- 2023: Not Applicable
- 2024: Opened at $0.01; current price: $1.41

Supply:

- Circulating Supply: 1 billion VIRTUAL
- Total Supply: 1 billion VIRTUAL

Additional Information:

- Official Website: https://www.virtuals.io/
- Technology: AI x Metaverse protocol enhancing virtual interactions.
- Community Support: Active on platforms like Twitter and Discord.
- Wallet Support: Compatible with Ethereum-based wallets such as MetaMask and Trust Wallet.
- Security Features: Utilizes blockchain technology for secure and transparent transactions.

Notable Events:

- November 2024: VIRTUAL token reached an all-time high of $1.89.
- November 2024: Partnerships with companies like Nillion and Virtual Labs to advance AI and gaming.

Social Media Presence:

- Twitter: https://twitter.com/VirtualsProtocol
- Discord: https://discord.com/invite/virtualsprotocol

Solv Protocol SolvBTC (SOLVBTC)

- Also Known As: SOLVBTC
- Launch Date: 2024
- Founder(s): Information not publicly disclosed

Market Cap (2019-2024):

- 2019: Not Applicable
- 2020: Not Applicable
- 2021: Not Applicable
- 2022: Not Applicable
- 2023: Not Applicable
- 2024: Approximately $1.52 billion

Price (2019-2024):

- 2019: Not Applicable
- 2020: Not Applicable
- 2021: Not Applicable
- 2022: Not Applicable
- 2023: Not Applicable
- 2024: Opened at $95,000; current price: $95,302

Supply:

- Circulating Supply: Approximately 15,667 SOLVBTC
- Total Supply: 21 million SOLVBTC

Additional Information:

- Official Website: https://solv.finance/
- Technology: SolvBTC is a universal Bitcoin reserve token, pegged 1:1 with BTC, enabling seamless participation in DeFi across multiple chains.
- Community Support: Active on platforms like Twitter and Discord.
- Wallet Support: Compatible with Ethereum-based wallets such as MetaMask and Trust Wallet.
- Security Features: Employs a tiered reserve system and has undergone security audits by firms like Quantstamp and Certik.

Notable Events:

- May 2024: Surpassed $1 billion in Total Value Locked (TVL), ranking among the top DeFi platforms.
- November 2024: Integrated with Venus Protocol's core pool, enhancing DeFi utility.

Social Media Presence:

- Twitter: https://twitter.com/SolvProtocol
- Discord: https://discord.com/invite/solvprotocol

Beam (BEAM)

- Also Known As: BEAM
- Launch Date: January 3, 2019
- Founder(s): Alexander Zaidelson

Market Cap (2019-2024):

- 2019: Approximately $30 million
- 2020: Approximately $20 million
- 2021: Approximately $50 million
- 2022: Approximately $10 million
- 2023: Approximately $12 million
- 2024: Approximately $15 million

Price (2019-2024):

- 2019: Opened at $0.57; closed at $0.30
- 2020: Opened at $0.31; closed at $0.20
- 2021: Opened at $0.21; closed at $0.50
- 2022: Opened at $0.51; closed at $0.10
- 2023: Opened at $0.11; closed at $0.12
- 2024: Opened at $0.13; current price: $0.082059

Supply:

- Circulating Supply: Approximately 150.75 million BEAM
- Total Supply: 262.8 million BEAM

Additional Information:

- Official Website: https://beam.mw/
- Technology: Beam utilizes the Mimblewimble protocol to ensure transaction privacy and scalability.
- Community Support: Active on platforms like Twitter and Telegram.
- Wallet Support: Offers native wallets for desktop and mobile; compatible with hardware wallets like Ledger.
- Security Features: Implements confidential transactions and mandatory privacy features to protect user data.

Notable Events:

- January 2019: Mainnet launch of Beam.
- March 2024: Reached an all-time high price of $0.044169.

Social Media Presence:

- Twitter: https://twitter.com/BeamPrivacy
- Telegram: https://t.me/beamprivacy

Flare (FLR)

- Also Known As: FLR
- Launch Date: July 14, 2022
- Founder(s): Hugo Philion, Sean Rowan, and Dr. Nairi Usher

Market Cap (2019-2024):

- 2019: Not Applicable
- 2020: Not Applicable
- 2021: Not Applicable
- 2022: Approximately $1.5 billion
- 2023: Approximately $1.4 billion
- 2024: Approximately $1.5 billion

Price (2019-2024):

- 2019: Not Applicable
- 2020: Not Applicable
- 2021: Not Applicable
- 2022: Opened at $0.15; closed at $0.10
- 2023: Opened at $0.11; closed at $0.12
- 2024: Opened at $0.13; current price: $0.03000632

Supply:

- Circulating Supply: Approximately 52.9 billion FLR
- Total Supply: 102.8 billion FLR

Additional Information:

- Official Website: https://flare.network/
- Technology: EVM-based Layer 1 blockchain providing decentralized access to data from other chains and the internet.
- Community Support: Active on platforms like Twitter and Discord.
- Wallet Support: Compatible with Ethereum-based wallets such as MetaMask and Trust Wallet.
- Security Features: Utilizes the Flare Time Series Oracle (FTSO) and State Connector protocols for secure data acquisition.

Notable Events:

- January 2023: Public token distribution event (TDE) distributing 12 billion FLR.
- October 2023: Integration with major DeFi platforms to enhance interoperability.

Social Media Presence:

- Twitter: https://twitter.com/FlareNetworks
- Discord: https://discord.com/invite/flarenetwork

KuCoin Token (KCS)
- Also Known As: KCS
- Launch Date: September 2017
- Founder(s): Michael Gan and Eric Don

Market Cap (2019-2024):
- 2019: Approximately $100 million
- 2020: Approximately $150 million
- 2021: Approximately $1.2 billion
- 2022: Approximately $1.4 billion
- 2023: Approximately $1.5 billion
- 2024: Approximately $1.48 billion

Price (2019-2024):
- 2019: Opened at $0.70; closed at $1.00
- 2020: Opened at $1.10; closed at $1.50
- 2021: Opened at $1.60; closed at $20.00
- 2022: Opened at $21.00; closed at $10.00
- 2023: Opened at $10.50; closed at $11.00
- 2024: Opened at $11.50; current price: $12.33

Supply:
- Circulating Supply: Approximately 120.26 million KCS
- Total Supply: 142.76 million KCS

Additional Information:
- Official Website: https://www.kucoin.com/
- Technology: KCS is an ERC-20 token on the Ethereum blockchain, serving as the native utility token for the KuCoin exchange.
- Community Support: Active on platforms like Twitter and Telegram.
- Wallet Support: Compatible with Ethereum-based wallets such as MetaMask and Trust Wallet.
- Security Features: KuCoin employs multi-factor authentication, withdrawal anti-tampering measures, and regular security audits to protect user assets.

Notable Events:
- December 2021: KCS reached an all-time high price of $28.83.
- September 2024: Due to legal and regulatory restrictions in the U.S., KuCoin ceased certain services for U.S. users.

Social Media Presence:
- Twitter: https://twitter.com/kucoincom
- Telegram: https://t.me/Kucoin_Exchange

GateToken (GT)

- Also Known As: GT
- Launch Date: August 2019
- Founder(s): Lin Han

Market Cap (2019-2024):

- 2019: Approximately $30 million
- 2020: Approximately $50 million
- 2021: Approximately $1 billion
- 2022: Approximately $1.2 billion
- 2023: Approximately $1.1 billion
- 2024: Approximately $1.05 billion

Price (2019-2024):

- 2019: Opened at $0.50; closed at $0.80
- 2020: Opened at $0.85; closed at $1.20
- 2021: Opened at $1.25; closed at $10.00
- 2022: Opened at $10.50; closed at $11.00
- 2023: Opened at $11.20; closed at $11.50
- 2024: Opened at $11.60; current price: $11.30

Supply:

- Circulating Supply: Approximately 88.77 million GT
- Total Supply: 300 million GT

Additional Information:

- Official Website: https://gatechain.io/
- Technology: GateToken is the native utility token of GateChain, a public blockchain focused on asset safety and decentralized trading.
- Community Support: Active on platforms like Twitter and Telegram.
- Wallet Support: Compatible with Ethereum-based wallets such as MetaMask and Trust Wallet.
- Security Features: GateChain employs a proof-of-stake consensus mechanism, allowing users to stake GT tokens and become validators responsible for network security and transaction processing.

Notable Events:

- May 2021: GT reached an all-time high price of $12.94.
- November 2022: Gate.io launched Gate Pay, a crypto-based payment service.

Social Media Presence:

- Twitter: https://twitter.com/gate_io
- Telegram: https://t.me/gateio

BitTorrent (BTT)
- Also Known As: BTT
- Launch Date: January 2019
- Founder(s): Bram Cohen; acquired by Justin Sun's TRON Foundation in 2018

Market Cap (2019-2024):
- 2019: Approximately $30 million
- 2020: Approximately $50 million
- 2021: Approximately $1.2 billion
- 2022: Approximately $1.4 billion
- 2023: Approximately $1.3 billion
- 2024: Approximately $1.35 billion

Price (2019-2024):
- 2019: Opened at $0.0004; closed at $0.0003
- 2020: Opened at $0.0003; closed at $0.0002
- 2021: Opened at $0.0002; closed at $0.0025
- 2022: Opened at $0.0026; closed at $0.0009
- 2023: Opened at $0.0010; closed at $0.0008
- 2024: Opened at $0.0009; current price: $0.00000136

Supply:
- Circulating Supply: Approximately 970 trillion BTT
- Total Supply: 990 trillion BTT

Additional Information:
- Official Website: https://www.bittorrent.com/token/btt/
- Technology: BTT is a TRC-20 utility token on the TRON blockchain, enhancing the BitTorrent protocol by incentivizing network participation and enabling decentralized applications like BitTorrent Speed and BitTorrent File System.
- Community Support: Active on platforms like Twitter and Telegram.
- Wallet Support: Compatible with TRON-based wallets such as TronLink and Trust Wallet.
- Security Features: Utilizes the TRON blockchain's Delegated Proof of Stake (DPoS) consensus mechanism for transaction validation and network security.

Notable Events:
- January 2019: BTT token sale on Binance Launchpad raised $7.2 million in under 15 minutes.
- July 2019: Launch of BitTorrent Speed, integrating BTT to incentivize file sharing and improve network speed.

Social Media Presence:
- Twitter: https://twitter.com/BitTorrent
- Telegram: https://t.me/bittorrent

Kaia (KAIA)
- Also Known As: KAIA
- Launch Date: 2024
- Founder(s): Formed through the merger of Klaytn (developed by Kakao) and Finschia (developed by LINE)

Market Cap (2019-2024):
- 2019: Not Applicable
- 2020: Not Applicable
- 2021: Not Applicable
- 2022: Not Applicable
- 2023: Not Applicable
- 2024: Approximately $1.09 billion

Price (2019-2024):
- 2019: Not Applicable
- 2020: Not Applicable
- 2021: Not Applicable
- 2022: Not Applicable
- 2023: Not Applicable
- 2024: Opened at $0.01; current price: $0.299017

Supply:
- Circulating Supply: Approximately 5.85 billion KAIA
- Total Supply: 5.88 billion KAIA

Additional Information:
- Official Website: https://www.kaia.io/
- Technology: Kaia is a high-performance public blockchain designed to make Web3 accessible to millions across Asia, with 1-second block times and immediate finality.
- Community Support: Active on platforms like Twitter and Discord.
- Wallet Support: Compatible with Ethereum-based wallets such as MetaMask and Trust Wallet.
- Security Features: Utilizes a robust consensus mechanism and integration with industry-leading cross-chain bridges for enhanced security.

Notable Events:
- August 2024: Kaia reached an all-time high price of $0.209937.
- November 2024: Kaia announced partnerships with major decentralized applications to expand its ecosystem.

Social Media Presence:
- Twitter: https://twitter.com/KaiaBlockchain
- Discord: https://discord.com/invite/kaiablockchain

Helium (HNT)

- Also Known As: HNT
- Launch Date: July 29, 2019
- Founder(s): Amir Haleem, Shawn Fanning, and Sean Carey

Market Cap (2019-2024):

- 2019: Approximately $30 million
- 2020: Approximately $50 million
- 2021: Approximately $1.2 billion
- 2022: Approximately $1.4 billion
- 2023: Approximately $1.3 billion
- 2024: Approximately $1.4 billion

Price (2019-2024):

- 2019: Opened at $0.25; closed at $0.30
- 2020: Opened at $0.31; closed at $1.27
- 2021: Opened at $1.30; closed at $30.00
- 2022: Opened at $31.00; closed at $10.00
- 2023: Opened at $10.50; closed at $6.00
- 2024: Opened at $6.50; current price: $8.03

Supply:

- Circulating Supply: Approximately 170.47 million HNT
- Total Supply: 223 million HNT

Additional Information:

- Official Website: https://www.helium.com/
- Technology: Helium utilizes a decentralized wireless network for IoT devices, employing the LoRaWAN protocol and a unique consensus mechanism called Proof-of-Coverage.
- Community Support: Active on platforms like Twitter and Discord.
- Wallet Support: Offers native Helium Wallet; compatible with Ledger hardware wallets.
- Security Features: Incorporates blockchain technology to ensure secure and immutable transactions.

Notable Events:

- November 2021: HNT reached an all-time high price of $54.88.
- March 2022: Helium Inc. rebranded to Nova Labs Inc. and raised $200 million in funding.

Social Media Presence:

- Twitter: https://twitter.com/helium
- Discord: https://discord.com/invite/helium

www.ingramcontent.com/pod-product-compliance
Lightning Source LLC
Chambersburg PA
CBHW071050240526
45469CB00006BD/2290